The D⬤NUT Book

The DNUT Book

The Whole Story in Words, Pictures & Outrageous Tales

SALLY LEVITT STEINBERG

America's Donut Princess

With a foreword by Jane and Michael Stern

Storey Publishing

The mission of Storey Publishing is to serve our customers by
publishing practical information that encourages
personal independence in harmony with the environment.

Edited by Dianne Cutillo and Andrea Dodge
Designed by Wendy Palitz
Cover photographs and original interior photography
by Zeva Oelbaum
Styled by Mary Placek
A list of additional photo credits appears on page 178.
A list of text credits appears on page 177.
Text production by Jennifer Jepson Smith and Melanie Jolicoeur
Indexed by Susan Olason

Storey books are available for special premium and promotional uses and for customized editions.
For further information, please call 1-800-793-9396.

Printed in China by R. R. Donnelley
10 9 8 7

Library of Congress Cataloging-in-Publication Data

Steinberg, Sally Levitt.
  The donut book / Sally Levitt Steinberg.
    p. cm.
  ISBN 978-1-58017-548-7 (pb : alk. paper)
  1. Doughnuts. I. Title.
TX770.D67S74 2004
641.8'353—dc22

2004014569

CONTENTS

To DML,
the Incomparable Donut King

FOREWORD

by Jane & Michael Stern

If any single-serving pastry deserves a biography, it's the donut. Cupcakes, biscuits, muffins, Danishes, and sticky buns are all worthy of attention, but none has the personality of a donut. It is an all-day snack of cops and truckers, the traditional sugar splurge at church-basement meetings of Alcoholics Anonymous, and the only proper snack at autumn cider-pressing parties. Like ice cream, it is happy food, good for a pig-out to eradicate depression any time of day, and coffee's best friend in the morning.

While it is perfectly at home in a blue-collar lunch pail, the donut dresses up to the nines, too — with multicolored sprinkles, jelly filling, glazes, and frosting. A well-made one is perfectly simple and simply perfect, its curving crisp surface as primal as a sweet Möbius strip, its insides a tunnel of tender dough packing all the pleasure of cake with the added thrill of deep frying. Even a mediocre donut, warm from the kettle, is a wicked treat.

Because it is such an honest, satisfying thing to eat, the donut has served as a national symbol through wars, hot and cold, and the Great Depression. Let the Russkies eat their black bread smeared with lard; leave heavy-centered bismarcks to the Germans and dainty brioches to the French. We'll have dunkable democracy, donuts by the dozen, thank you very much. In the Great War, American doughboys overseas were known to chant, "We want donuts!"; and in recent years the donut has handsomely survived the onslaught of such trendy pastry arrivistes as croissants and scones. As impervious to low-carb-diet dogma as to calorie-counting regimens of earlier times, the donut remains quintessential comfort food that only a killjoy nutrition warden couldn't love.

God bless Sally Levitt Steinberg, whose grandfather was the Henry Ford of donuts, and who has made donuts her muse, her inamorato, her literary mission. In this epic volume, she has created nothing less than the donut's official hagiography. Her command of the subject and her unrivaled passion for it make *The Donut Book* a blockbuster read with irresistible charisma. As donut lovers ourselves, we fairly wallowed in the bounty of delicious information that packs every page. The recipes are priceless, and the book's account of America's top donut bakeries is a Roadfood treasure.

The story of the donut in America begins with the arrival of the Dutch in the 17th century, and it becomes a sweet refrain through the nation's history. Ms. Steinberg tells its story with such vigor that a reader will never again think of the donut as a modest hunk of pastry. It is a reflection of culture and current events; it is a vivid presence in literature and art; it has inspired cartoons, great quotations, donut ditties, and etiquette arguments. No other single food we know could command the kind of awe given up in these pages, for as Sally Levitt Steinberg so convincingly portrays it, the donut is an edible Rosetta Stone of our time. Its story is here told with such enthusiasm that one cannot help but come away from *The Donut Book* a true believer.

DONUTS
NOW & FOREVER

What do the world's greatest chefs and the world's fastest food shops, presidents and the homeless, coffee breaks and the entertainment industry's fanciest parties have in common? Donuts! Donuts have become one of America's It foods.

Donuts are now.

Donuts are old.

They have been here since biblical times. The universe shares their shape, say cosmologists. They are an American symbol, although they are eaten in India as well as Indiana.

They are part of American history — Native American braves shot arrows through them, a whaling captain rammed one onto the ship's wheel to invent the hole, World War I soldiers ate them in trenches and wanted more. My grandfather Adolph Levitt was a poor Russian immigrant who bought into a bakery in Harlem, New York, and heard the soldiers asking for donuts. First, he fried them in a kettle in the bakery window. Long lines formed outside. Later he patented a donut-making machine and put it in the bakery window and then in Times Square. It was a sensation. He sold the machines, and then created the Mayflower brand of mixes and shops, named after the Pilgrim ship. He had become a proud American.

DONUTS ARE NEW

Donuts are "discovered" every day — witness Krispy Kreme, a new monument of American popular culture, and its trancelike effect on people standing in line all night at store openings. Patriotism has grown following 9/11, and with it the desire for American foods and symbols. Donuts are undergoing a resurgence. There is the culinary versatility of the donut, from simple to regal. There is the cultural versatility of the donut, from lowest-common-denominator cop snack to rarefied fancy dessert. Donuts made of organic ingredients, green tea donuts at an elegant New York restaurant — these are examples of the New Donut.

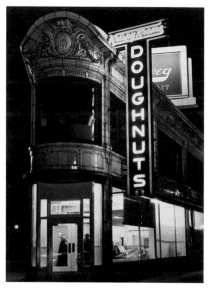

Since *The Donut Book* appeared in its first incarnation in 1987, there have been important developments. Mark Isreal's Doughnut Plant is now New York's most famous donut shop, with handmade donuts composed of organic farmers' market ingredients. His rose petal donuts have real rose petals on them! Bursting out of their status as pop culture symbol, donuts have entered higher life and art, served as dessert in fancy restaurants and painted by masters. Once, no fine restaurant would serve donuts for dessert. The biggest change in donuts as food is that there is now activity and competition in just that area. Donuts are emerging from their niche into the ethereal realms of haute cuisine, the hallowed precincts of elite temples of gastronomy. My grandfather lifted the lowly fried cake out of the frying pan. Now it is jumping back in, going from mass-produced everyman snack, the "poor man's rich food," to handcrafted, architectural dessert. The "Wonderful Almost Human Automatic Donut Machine" has ruled America for three quarters of a century. It is now ceding pride of place, or at least shoving over, to make room for the newly elevated high and mighty donut, a chef-made creation.

The new fancy dessert donut is a riff on this popular food, a takeoff, elegant and tasting great. These donuts are filled with fresh cream or accompanied by dipping sauce (dunking transmuted?). The fancy donut has a humorous side, a little bit tongue-in-cheek, and it makes people feel good, as donuts have always done. Fancy donuts reach all the way to Paris in the hands of the great French chef Alain Ducasse, who has six Michelin stars and a gourmet shop there with . . . donuts for sale!

Donuts have even become wedding cakes. In *People Weekly,* it says, "What really caught the attention of the 175 guests at the . . . nuptials . . . was the wedding cake. No butter cream frosting, no sculpted-sugar curlicues, just 120 Krispy Kreme glazed doughnuts stacked into a 4-ft.-tall pyramid, decorated with edible pansies and topped off with traditional bride-and-groom figurines. 'The cake . . . was the hit of the wedding. People tore it apart so fast, there were almost injuries.'"

Donuts are all over the electronic media — on thousands of Web sites, in the lingo of punk e-zines, in skateboarding lore. Homer Simpson's love of donuts is well known to TV watchers, and his infectious exclamation, "Mmmmm, donuts!" is its own pop litany. The Simpsons and their donuts have become a cult, with a whole industry in Simpson

Web sites and donut trinkets and posters and other paraphernalia. And donuts are showing up in the realm of fine art. They were served at the 2003 Art Show, the annual art fair gathering galleries from all over the world to display their works at the New York Armory.

DONUTS ARE PERENNIAL. DONUTS ARE FOREVER.

What other food has its own philosophical motto, like the one that tells you to "Keep Your Eye Upon the Doughnut"? What other food could inspire a Zen meditation called "Mystical and Metaphysical Qualities of an Average but Unknown Donut"? Donuts are in the cosmos — in orbits, in black holes, and in the shape of the universe, the torus.

Donuts are still the favorite food of cops and presidents and church suppers. The link between politics and donuts continues. Bill Clinton loves donuts so much that he ordered dozens for the White House, even going out in the middle of the night for them. Todd Purdum of the *New York Times* writes of the "nominating process, with its quadrennial hopscotch, from Iowa's pork tenderloins to New Hampshire's doughnuts . . ."

Donuts are always in the news and the public eye as well as in mouths and stomachs.

In 2003, ABC News did a segment called "The Sweet Success of Donuts." It pointed out that the "donut . . . is apparently more popular than ever."

The program noted that donut shops are "the fastest-growing dining segment in the food industry." One regular customer said, "I need something to relieve some stress and I guess eating a donut is the right thing to do. Before the gym!"

The newscaster ended by saying that he feels sorry for bagels.

Donuts are lasting, partly because they are a constant source of fun, and perhaps because they even have a spiritual side. A *New Yorker* cartoon, titled "Middle School Crisis," features one student saying to another, "I'll trade you my numb acceptance of a bleak and joyless future plus my crushing feeling of irredeemable loss for your chocolate-sprinkled doughnut." The donut reaches spiritual heights in the movie *Pieces of April*. April's dysfunctional family stops at a Krispy Kreme to get some donuts before Thanksgiving dinner, which will be cooked by the black sheep/non-cook, April. Her mother says to the donut seller, "We'll take an extra dozen glazed." Later the mother purrs over the donut, "How could anyone not believe in God?"

What would your last wish be if you knew you were going to depart from the earth? I have heard more than one person mention donuts as the choice for this honor, the final delicacy, without even being asked.

As Tevye said in *Fiddler on the Roof,* "On the other hand . . . ": Let us not forget that donuts have their downside, and that is perennial too. Donuts are often used as the image in discussions of weight gain and bad eating habits. In a recent mention in the *New York Times* of the expanding waistlines of Europeans, the accompanying photo is of the new Krispy Kreme counter at Harrods department store in London. In an article in the *New York Times*, George Hochman writes, "In his quest to reach the age of 143, Michael A. Sherman is making his peace with doughnuts." However, in a new book called *The Jelly Donut Diet,* Judge Lawrence Grey deflates some of America's sanctities, nutritional correctness included, arguing that a jelly donut a day works because it provides satisfaction.

Linda Neville is an American original. She fries the donuts after her husband makes them in their North Adams,

Massachusetts, shop, Neville's Do-Nut Shop, which has been there for 53 years. "My husband is the baker, I'm the baker's helper," she says. "He does the crullers. It is a skill to make them turn around and twirl."

Linda has become something of a donut philosopher and fountain of donut lore, through her experience in donuts and in education. She loves the metaphorical and philosophical reach of donuts. She says that for her senior seminar thesis,

she hit upon the concept of the donut hole as passageway, as a metaphor for the search for national identity in postcolonial societies. "So I was frying maybe my five hundredth donut," she says, "and there's all these donut shapes there — though it looks like there's nothing in the center, maybe it's really a passageway. When you take a journey, you're not always sure what's on the other side. The idea is that you definitely need the storytellers who travel around to the villages, so it's the concept of going around the donut, not through the hole, and sharing the stories."

Linda tells her students about making donuts. "When I teach, they know I am the donut shop lady," she says. "The thing about having a donut shop, it's like fieldwork for me. I use what I do here — skills and hours and all that — in my teaching." She has the police coming in — "You see what they have to deal with, and they take some comfort food." She and a Chinese worker in her shop swapped recipes in October, when the Chinese go out and watch the moon and Americans have National Donut Month. And one of her students likened the story of Rumpelstiltskin spinning straw into gold to making donuts out of wheat, also a kind of grass, and working all night to create a product that you make money with.

In her own version of sharing the storytelling, Linda teaches reading and study skills at the Massachusetts College of Liberal Arts (she says to me, "What you have compiled is my textbook"). She also has the private donut library in town. "I was collecting anything that had to do with donuts. I am the donut book library here." There's *The Donut Book*, and the others are children's books. And that's how the publisher of Storey Publishing came to borrow the original edition of this book and to see that, as Linda says, "it's got so many things that relate to other things but using the donuts as the symbol. It's like there's physics, everything, it could be anything. It's about donuts, but throughout it's talking about a sort of philosophy of life too — see, I'm going to get philosophical on you. A donut is eaten by anyone and everyone. So the whole idea of a donut . . . This is my inspiration, this book has all that I live with and it all links together, that's the fun part of it."

So it is fitting that a donut shop lady who is also a teacher with a philosophical bent and a person who values storytelling and the multifaceted life of donuts serves as the "passageway" to the new *Donut Book*, as it rides the wave of donut resurrection and proves the everlastingness of donuts. In an episode of *The Simpsons*, a runaway monorail train is saved from destruction by meeting up with a pile of donuts. The accompanying comment: "Donuts. Is there anything they can't do?"

Now and forever, old and new, ephemeral and eternal, sophisticated and basic, spiritual and comical, universal and American, pop culture and metaphysical, healthy or junk, grub or gourmet fare, donuts are us, U.S. and beyond.

To quote from *Homer Price*, a popular children's book by Robert McCloskey, with the donut machine on the cover as the focus of the story, donuts keep "right on a comin', an' a comin', an' a comin'."

The author's grandfather Adolph Levitt, who invented the donut machine.

One

ONCE UPON A TIME

It's true I'm not loyal to baseball, hot dogs, Coke, pretzels, and so forth. "So? How could you be American?" they ask. In defense, I insist that, while I may not be an eater of franks in bleachers, when it comes to food, my heritage entitles me to a place in American history. My grandfather invented the donut machine. He made donuts America's snack, part of office breaks, Halloween parties with donuts on strings, donut-plattered political rallies. Donuts are basic American equipment.

I come from immigrants who crossed the sea in steerage to flee persecution. They fled to the Midwest, then fled that land to fry cakes in a pot in Harlem, and then made a machine for that cake people loved. They got donuts out of the frying pans of prairie women and into coffee shops and onto Coney Island; they got them into prisons, where inmates barter them for cigarettes, and into the White House for a contest to see which senator could eat the most. They got donuts in lights, on Broadway, on highways, their portrait in neon, on billboards.

got to be the granddaughter of donuts, a donut Pocahontas. I am part of the clanking of machines cutting rings of dough, the bubbling of fat frying the rings, the sugary smell of factory kitchens clouded white with donut flour, where rows of even donuts puff proudly.

My friends knew that my grandfather was the Donut King. It was like being the descendant of Old King Cole.

On the first day of first grade, I wore a red-and-green-plaid dress above my patent leather Mary Janes and white socks, and on my white collar I wore something that made me different. A pin. It was yellow and brown plastic, in the shape of a cup of steaming coffee, with a donut poised above, ready for dunking. This meant I was a genuine Donut Dunker, a member of the National Dunking Association.

Though my ancestors did not come over with the Pilgrims, I can lay claim to a Mayflower in my past, even if it is the name of the chain of donut shops my grandfather started. Donuts as American as the *Mayflower*, in icing costumes as pink as ballet tutus, as green as leprechauns. We always had boxes of Mayflower donuts, complete with an image of a square-rigged ship, lying around our kitchen. I thought donuts were important, and I saw I was not the only one.

I saw the lines of people outside the Mayflower shops waiting for donuts coming out hot from the machine — confetti-colored or fuzzy cinnamon brown or snow-white powdered sugar donuts. I saw customers with their hands behind their backs, mouths waving to catch the donut, like seals in the zoo trying to catch the ball. Donuts must be worth it, I concluded as a child, or grown-ups would not stoop to such foolishness.

And then there was the motto on the Mayflower box. It was within a quaint insignia of two men dressed as old-fashioned jesters, facing away from each other, my grandfather's motto in curly, old-style print between them:

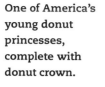

One of America's young donut princesses, complete with donut crown.

MAYFLOWER DOUGHNUTS
Summer-afternoon crowd at the national headquarters of Mayflower Doughnuts (above) and Danny Donut (right).

**As you ramble on thru Life, Brother,
Whatever be your Goal,
Keep your Eye upon the Doughnut
And not upon the Hole.**

One of the jesters is smiling at a fat donut with a small hole and the other is frowning at a thin donut encircling a large, airy hole. My grandfather found this motto, the Optimist's Creed, as it is called, inside a cheap picture frame he bought in a dime store. He adopted the saying as his philosophy of life. Donuts, I thought, must be fairly basic if they had made it into a motto where life's choice was drawn in the shape of a donut.

Calico scallops and bighorn sheep made the stamp, the eagle made the emblem, and the donut made the church supper and cop stop, the Native American legend and the motto. Donuts made their way across the country like pioneers in Conestoga wagons, all the way from Maine to Times Square to Hollywood. They have inspired tales about seafarers, cartoons about dreams, Burns and Allen comedy routines. They have invaded hobo lingo and Hemingway stories. Native American lore tells of a trade of donuts for a hostage Pilgrim wife. Donuts fed the famished in Great Depression days, and now they are free food for the homeless. There was the Donut Tower of the first World's Fair, and there was the National Dunking Association, with tens of thousands of official dunkers led by Red Skelton and Jimmy Durante. Admiral Byrd took donuts to the polar regions, and Eddie Cantor took them to the movies.

Since World War I, when soldiers and Salvation Army women fried donuts in garbage cans and stacked them on bayonets, this beloved object has been part of the eternal snackability of America, belonging to grassroots as well as fast-food culture. This is America, where you can play Donut Ring Toss, where Texas church youth made the biggest donut ever (74 pounds' worth), and where four women over 65 competed in a donut-making contest in Maine and no good donuts resulted. While pasta and tacos fight for neon, the old standby, the donut, eaten on the park bench, anchors the American to the soil. It is the food of the heartland.

I have been all over the country searching out donuts. I have wandered around the country where the Pottawatomie met fur trappers on their journeys up the Milwaukee River in canoes. I have been to Emporia, Kansas, miles out into the prairies, watching donuts travel on conveyor belts and eating chicken-fried steak in the Emporia American Legion Club.

The art and etiquette of donut dunking.

Like Mother *used* to make

WARTIME DONUTS
For soldiers in wartime, donuts have always been reminders of hearth and home. Below is an unusual donut shop with an out-of-the-ordinary customer.

I hear donut stories wherever I go. A psychiatrist tells me he and his cousin get a bag of two dozen every Sunday and eat the whole lot right away. A taxi driver tells me of growing up in Providence eating donuts — the greasy kind, he tells me fondly — each morning at six, before everyone else was awake. Donut nostalgia for the compact, holey meal in itself — breakfast, lunch, snack, or dessert.

Donuts are everywhere. Their eyes stare up at me from a tray at a doctor's office. On a ledge in a gas station I see a half-eaten donut, a fossil. People are walking around the city streets on New Year's Eve with donuts in their hands for warmth. In a modern painting, a donut rests on the edge of a sewing machine.

I visited a donut plant to see donuts in the making. After weaving past gyrating, oversize mixing bowls, I entered the testing area, where rows of donuts came off conveyor belts. The fresh, sweet, mouthwatering aroma hit hard. As I started to snatch one from a bin, on top I saw a damp, half-smoked cigar, lending the donuts the stale stench of a poolroom. So much for visions of donuts instead of breakfast.

A rumor circulates of a donut poster in the Paris métro, so I prowl for weeks trying to find it. Finally, there it is, in Montmartre, where Impressionists roamed the alleys, where sidewalk art jostles the accordion player, where singers from the provinces vie for customers in the night spots, and where guests drink kir and join in the chorus of songs handed down from medieval France. In the shadow of Sacré-Coeur is a blue and yellow poster of American donuts.

In a department store in Tokyo, two Japanese men, Mr. Fukushima and Mr. Kawakami, fry donuts with chopsticks in a cauldron of fat, next to seaweed and sake. The crowd thickens, so you cannot see the donuts. Amid silks and fragile teacups and Zen rock formations and fine black ash heaped to heat green leaves for the tea ceremony, the Japanese eat donuts on Tokyo's Fifth Avenue, the Ginza, behind rice paper screens, after lunches of yakitori chicken.

Donuts have been my corner of American life ever since I can remember. Donuts were around me all the time, beautiful ones in pink jackets or with red and silver sprinkles. But people disparage the donut, take it for granted without looking. Donuts are common, maybe, but a common favorite. Besides, how can something that is the lowest common denominator be unimportant? People eat donuts in a shop; a girl places them on a tray. Does the girl or the cop or the nurse stop to look, to ask why people love this thing, joke about it? Why does the donut invite, tickle, please, suggest? What is this ring I'm ruining by biting? Why does a monk meditate on it? The donut we have in hand we take for granted, until one day we notice. Noticing is what we are here for.

Randy's Donuts

When you see the donut, it's time to land! say pilots coming into Los Angeles. You can't miss the Big Donut strutting astride America's most visible donut shop, Randy's.

Outsize and outrageous, funny and inviting and bigger than life, that donut could be nowhere but here.

The Big Donut calls from L.A. roads to the world, a visual lingua franca. A French farmer tilling fields of sunflowers in Provence wears its T-shirt. So near and yet so far. Showcasing L.A.'s exotic in-your-face culture, beckoning travelers, Randy's is the cover image for the Frommer and Rough travel guides.

Russ Wendell created Randy's in the 1950s as part of the new freeway culture and its roadside architecture, with supersize product images to ensnare America's mobile. Randy's, the world's first fast-food drive-in, for life in the fast lane, serving donuts made fresh all day under the Big Donut, donuts consistently cited among L.A.'s best. "People could come in pajamas and rollers if they couldn't sleep. They wouldn't have to get out of the car," say brothers Ron and Larry Weintraub, the current owners.

Randy's has appeared in a Singapore newspaper, in a movie with Richard Gere, and in ads for Delta Dental and Depends. A midget on a flying trapeze and Santa's reindeer have flown through the Big Donut's hole.

Unforgettable image, irresistible donuts.

What could be more elemental than a circle of dough? What could be more dignified? That's why a Zen monk writes a meditation on donuts, seeing eternity in them, seeing life and death, nothing and everything, heaven and earth. A donut sits on the heads of saints and angels. A donut in the woods, a circle of mushrooms, is a folk miracle, a "fairy ring." Donuts are the stuff of dreams. Jules Feiffer's donut dream has become a famous cartoon, a vision of a flight up a staircase to encounter a giant donut. Highbrow and low, serious and silly, ridiculous and sublime, the donut is food and thought and food for thought. The polymorphous donut, then, is not just what it seems to be. What is it? Is it art or science, food or folklore, joke or symbol, pop culture or myth, gimmick or life?

Some have wondered if the donut itself is art. Artists have painted donuts, sculpted them, even built them into monuments. But what about the donut on its own? Is the everyday donut a piece of cosmic art? A sort of

Graham Cracker Donuts

This recipe is from the *Herald Tribune Cookbook*.

Makes 2 dozen

- 1½ cups sifted all-purpose flour
- 4 teaspoons baking powder
- ¾ teaspoon salt
- 1 teaspoon grated nutmeg or ½ teaspoon cinnamon
- 1½ cups finely rolled graham cracker crumbs
- 2 tablespoons butter
- ⅔ cup granulated sugar
- 1 egg, beaten
- ⅔ cup milk
- Oil for deep frying
- Confectioners' sugar (optional)

1. Sift together flour, baking powder, salt, and nutmeg; stir in rolled cracker crumbs.

2. Cream butter; add sugar and egg, beating thoroughly; add flour-crumb mixture alternately with milk.

3. Turn out onto a floured board and roll to ¼ inch thick; cut with floured donut cutter.

4. Fry in hot, deep oil (360–370°F) for 2 to 3 minutes, or until they are lightly browned; drain on unglazed paper and roll in confectioners' sugar, if desired.

Greek temple of food? Perhaps the donut — as edible embodiment of the circle, to look at, to eat — is a kind of artistic accident of nature. Or are donuts mostly science, the attempt by humanity to create the shape in nature that is most fundamental in the heavens and on earth? Since the universe holds so many circles, one day humans would have wanted to invent an edible circle, according to the natural law of putting everything in the mouth.

Donuts are hard to pin down but easy to eat. They are fantasy and reality, jokes and ritual objects, symbols and sinkers. They are cosmological and biological. They are physical and metaphysical. They are beatific and they are ruinous. They are fattening. They are sublime. They are predictable and unexpected. They are folkloric. They are sexy. They are well rounded, even global. They are irreverent, but they are holey. And holy, the Zen monk said. And what choice does anyone have in life but to look at the donut or the hole?

Pazo Beignets with Catalan Cream

Eating is a sensual experience to people of the Mediterranean. Food is often eaten with the hands, abandoning the structure of the fork, knife, and spoon. Pazo embraces this tradition with its desserts. Beignets are casual, fun, and can be eaten right from the hand. Catalan cream, a rich and creamy dessert from Spain, is the perfect complement to the sugary beignets. *Makes 15 small beignets*

BEIGNETS

- 11 ounces milk
- ¾ cup shortening
- ¼ cup sugar
- ¼ cup cooked and mashed potato, cooled
- 1 vanilla bean, seeds scraped from pod
- ¼ ounce fresh yeast
- ¼ cup water
- 1 egg
- ¼ teaspoon pure vanilla extract
- 3½ cups all-purpose flour
- 1½ teaspoons salt
- ½ teaspoon baking powder
- Vegetable oil for frying

1. Combine the first five ingredients in a saucepan and warm until shortening melts. Allow to cool.

2. Combine the yeast, water, egg, and vanilla in a large bowl. Mix the flour, salt, and baking powder into the yeast mixture. Add the shortening mixture. Beat by hand or with an electric mixer until a dough is developed, 6 to 8 minutes. Cover the dough with plastic and allow to proof in a warm place until it doubles in size.

3. Once the dough has doubled, flour a work surface and roll the dough to desired thickness. Cover the dough and chill for approximately 1 hour. Meanwhile, spray pieces of parchment paper with nonstick cooking spray.

4. Once chilled, cut the dough into desired shapes and lay them on the parchment. Wrap with plastic and allow the dough to proof again in a warm place for 20 minutes.

5. While the dough is proofing, heat the vegetable oil to 375°F. Fry the beignets until golden brown. Serve immediately with Catalan Cream (recipe at right).

CATALAN CREAM

Makes approximately 15 (4-ounce) servings

14 egg yolks
2 (14-ounce) cans sweetened condensed milk
3½ cups Infused Water (see below)

1. Preheat the oven to 325°F.
2. Combine all the ingredients in a large bowl and mix well.
3. Strain ingredients through a fine mesh strainer into a large bowl.
4. Pour the mixture into 15 individual 4-ounce ramekins. Place ramekins in a deep roasting pan and fill pan two thirds high with hot water. Place roasting pan in oven.
5. Bake until set, approximately 15 minutes. The middle should jiggle a little bit but the edges should be set.
6. Chill in fridge for 4 to 6 hours. Serve chilled with warm beignets.

Infused Water
1 quart water
1 cinnamon stick
½ tablespoon fennel seeds, toasted and ground
Zest of ½ orange

Combine ingredients in a large saucepan and bring to a boil. Remove from heat and strain through a fine mesh strainer.

DONUTS ON THE BEACH

On the beach in St.-Tropez, France, Rahel, age three, eats a large rectangular donut with jelly squirts in it. She gets it from an African guy carrying the box of donuts on his head and calling, "Les beignets, framboise, chocolat," which is intoned in the lilt of an African tribal chant, a refrain from the bush or desert, in its own idiom, exotic, with a modality echoing far-off places, redolent donuts carried by the "chi chi guy" on the socialite beach where glitz reigns, Pucci bathing suits strut, and kids in Baby Dior eat doughy rectangles bigger than their faces and oozing red jam.

AN AMERICAN DREAM
How America Got the Donut
& a Donut King

My grandfather Adolph Levitt was not always the American Donut King, as they called him. He began as a village boy in Russia, son of a Jewish grain merchant. It all started when Uncle Jake, my grandfather's older brother, came to the New World to get away from anti-Jewish riots in Russia. He bought a pushcart, loaded it with dry goods, and dragged it across the Midwest and out to Oregon, hawking his wares — a button here, a zipper there. In a year Jake, the greenhorn with the wagon, had made enough money to bring his family across the sea.

He brought them to the middle of this vast new country. They became as American as the dwellers in the towns and plains of the American Midwest. In this land my grandfather, his parents, and his seven brothers and sisters came to roost.

In this New World my grandfather wanted to forget his past, the village of Pondiclia in Russia, a past full of what he called "no-goods" and "horse thieves." Like other Jewish immigrants of that era, he left his past so far behind that his children hardly knew anything about it. My father said he was amazed to learn that people could read back in that dark time.

My grandfather was eight in 1892, when he came to meet Jake in Milwaukee. Into this heavyset, sturdy city, my grandfather's mother brought her family of eight and her husband, who would die after a year, leaving her penniless. On the streets of Milwaukee, where hard work rules, children found work as newsboys. At age 10, after two years of American school, my grandfather had to quit to save pennies by selling papers to brothels. To educate himself, he read encyclopedias from cover to cover.

My grandfather began his new life in Wisconsin, taking on some of the toughness of the place, its spirit of readiness, because it was part of a land that was not quite finished. It was a country in the making, as he was in the making. He let go of his past and got for himself some of the energy and raw force of a new land. When he and his brother John were only 14 and 15, they went into the "mercantile business." Their plan was to put everything in the window, suits and hats and shoes. My grandfather was proud of his window displays; he knew people liked to stop to look at things in windows. He opened one store after another — hats and shoes and gloves and belts — on the streets of towns like Rhinelander, Wisconsin, and Hibbing, Minnesota, as well as Milwaukee. One after the other, the stores closed.

My grandfather, at 37, left the city of beer and ballrooms and billiard halls and headed

Adolph Levitt, the inventor of the donut machine, founded Mayflower Doughnuts.

An early machine in a bakery window had crowds lining up to watch.

east for New York, too poor to take his family with him and in disgrace among friends and relatives who had invested in his last unsuccessful dry-goods store. All he had was some "mad money" my grandmother had put away under mattresses for emergencies. She stashed away money in this way until her dying day, after the Donut Kingdom had reigned for decades, the days when she insisted on using her Golden Age Club pass for the movies and put up a fight if someone wouldn't let her in. The money allowed my grandfather to buy into a bakery chain at a time when the place of donuts was in a frying pan in the kitchen. In 1920, my grandfather met the soldiers returning from the war. The "doughboys" of World War I had the taste of donuts in their mouths, the donuts Salvation Army women had fried in garbage pails in France. Donuts became the rave of the trenches, filling bellies and warming hearts with

Norman Rockwell's magazine cover with wartime donut nostalgia.

the taste of home. The women could hardly keep the soldiers supplied. The association of donuts with soldiers continued into World War II as well, making a bridge to home, inspiring patriotism.

Johnny came marching home asking for donuts. The cries of the doughboys on a donut rampage rang across the countryside. My grandfather heard and saw to it that America got the donuts he knew it needed. He took a kettle and pushed it to the window of his bakery in Harlem and fried donuts in it. People loved to watch the donuts frying in the window, and they loved eating them. Pretty soon the crowd in front of the window was too large to get through; people wanted more donuts than the kettle in the bakeshop could fry.

My grandfather thought up the idea of a machine to make donuts, turning them automatically, getting rid of fumes from the open kettle with a fan to push them to the roof, and producing donuts in greater numbers for the crowds outside the window. One day, in the dining car of a train to Chicago, he sat next to an engineer. By way of making conversation, he told the engineer about the bakery and the lines outside the window. The engineer offered to sketch a machine and send it through the mail. He did, but the machine did not work. Together the men invented 11 more unworkable machines for making donuts, by trial and error, the way children invent impossible machines. The engineer built them in a one-man machine shop. Finally, the 12th try worked. It had cost $15,000 to make. In 1920 my grandfather put the machine in the bakery window so everyone could see the miraculous way to plop dough rings into fat, bathe them in oil, crisp them brown, flip them over, and cool the donuts on trays. People loved watching the

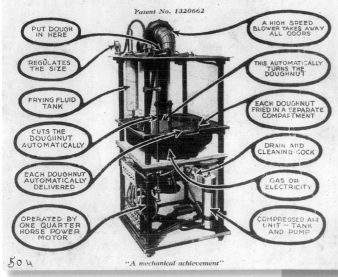

Patent No. 1320662

PUT DOUGH
IN HERE

A HIGH SPEED
BLOWER TAKES AWAY
ALL ODORS

REGULATES
THE SIZE

THIS AUTOMATICALLY
TURNS THE
DOUGHNUT

FRYING FLUID
TANK

EACH DOUGHNUT
FRIED IN A SEPARATE
COMPARTMENT

CUTS THE
DOUGHNUT
AUTOMATICALLY

DRAIN AND
CLEANING COCK

EACH DOUGHNUT
AUTOMATICALLY
DELIVERED

GAS OR
ELECTRICITY

OPERATED BY
ONE QUARTER
HORSE POWER
MOTOR

COMPRESSED AIR
UNIT — TANK
AND PUMP

504

"A mechanical achievement"

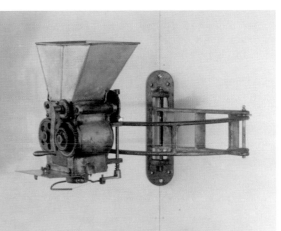

EARLY DONUT MACHINES

This drawing of a plan (above) is for an early machine that may or may not have worked. The hand-crank donut maker over a pot of oil (right) preceded the donut machine.

Wonderful Almost Human Automatic Donut Machine, as it was called, where dough went in and donuts streamed out. Bakers from all over came to buy machines for their bakeries. My grandfather sold 128 machines the first year. He paid the engineer for his help, and the engineer went his own way. In 1921 my grandfather made $250,000, enough to put the money back under my grandmother's mattress and have some left over.

Just as Jake had pushed his cart to everyone's door and sold with determination to get his family out of the Russian village, out of unrelenting oppression to be free in the New World, my grandfather pushed his donut

...the food hit
OF THE
**CENTURY of
PROGRESS**

*See them made
automatically
at the*

DOUGHNUT·EXHIBIT
1934 WORLD'S FAIR
near the 23rd St. entrance
C·H·I·C·A·G·O

DOUGHNUTS

machine to the window so everyone would see how it made donuts. Crowds pressed their noses against the window to watch the donuts boil and bubble in the fat. And my grandfather Adolph Levitt, formerly Yuda-levich, became the Donut King overnight, the American dream come true.

One by one, my grandfather and his donut men sold machines to people all over America. They sold them to small bakeries and to five-and-tens, to fairgrounds and beaches and amusement parks. They linked up with Max-well House coffee, opening coffee and donut shops, and with larger baking companies, selling their donuts under brand names like Ward and A&P.

Later my grandfather and his donut men pushed the machine to a window in Times Square, New York City. My grandfather, the village boy from Russia, put his machine under news ticker tapes, in lighted letters with a giant billboard mouth

DONUT PROGRESS
At the World's Fair in Chicago, machine-made donuts were on display for the first time. Below, right, the entrance to the Doughnut Hut.

blowing smoke rings with an outsize cigarette. In Times Square, buildings cut the horizon into block shapes and traffic streamed out of the grimy, shouting, brassy, sequined city and probably to the rest of the world. Nearby was Lindy's, the famous delicatessen, where donuts were dunked for the first time. And in the middle of this swirl of energy was a bakery with a machine spilling out donuts and blowing their aroma into the street. The machine was a sensation. It knotted New York traffic all over the city. Forests of craning necks and grabbing fists pressed into a human clot. The city sent its police force, sirens blaring, to the emergency, a Donut Emergency.

In the 1930s, donuts boomed while the country bowed its head under the weight of a tumbledown economy. For my grandfather, the Depression became an Elation. When he had started in business, people had called him in Yiddish the "guy with a few coppers" — he never made money. Now for a few coppers he sold donuts, at a time when people could afford only a few pennies, and the pennies streamed in. At first he counted them on his kitchen table. At the World's Fair many people saw the machine for the first time, ate its donuts, and wanted more donuts. My grandfather knew about the tired, the poor, slumped on the benches of Battery Park opposite the proud Statue of Liberty holding her torch. The poor man made the "poor man's cake."

In those days of breadlines, donuts became a staple for the working class, a dozen in wax paper for 15 cents. The workers at the donut company made them even when they had to melt down hard candy for sugar. In those days, the company took up trainloads of migrants from Tennessee to work in the plant. My grandfather developed an evangelical style to sell the donut in the middle of despair. People called him a "regular Billy Sunday" with his talent for rabble-rousing. He gathered flashy characters around him, like the one who wore wing collars and polka-dot ties and a handlebar mustache, like "an advance man in a circus." In those days my grandfather decreed that his workers would lunch with him every day at his favorite restaurant, Jansen-Wants-to-

One of the first "little" donut machines for small bakeries.

See-You. He smoked his Corona cigar, talked no business, and occasionally bellowed about not much: a sort of Mad Hatter's Tea Party Nonbusiness Lunch in Old New York.

My grandfather, they said, was a marketing genius. From the idea of putting things in windows, he went on to other tricks. He used names from American history: Lincoln for the machine, Mayflower for his donut shop chain. Realizing that the machines alone were not enough, since they were built like battleships to last for 25 years and chew up millions of pounds of mix, he got into making the mix and the flour. Then he started bakeries to make donuts, and restaurants where people could eat them, and advertising schemes to sell them.

Donuts were the way to the stars, the Hollywood stars. They took off from Times Square — where dunking caught on after Mae Murray, the actress, dropped a donut into her coffee at Lindy's by accident — for Hollywood. The National Dunking Association had Hollywood stars for its leaders — Red Skelton, Eddie Cantor, Zero Mostel, and Johnny Carson. Eddie Cantor starred in a movie alongside a donut machine.

Adolph rented machines to the Red Cross during World War II so the soldiers could have donuts. Three hundred machines on Clubmobiles and millions of pounds of donut mix went out to boost the morale of soldiers in wartime again. His company won the "A" award from the U.S. government — A for achievement, for supplying food to the armed services in the war.

My grandfather understood America in a way that people who grow up in its vast middle do, the real America between the jeweled coasts. He knew the donut filing home from France with the soldiers to be an American object, as American as the coasts and the plains, as American as he and his Russian brothers were as they grew up scrapping in the streets, as American as the donut warehouse in Brooklyn, which rubs elbows with Hasidic Jews with sidelocks and with Latinos eating chorizo.

He and his men did not give up until they had conquered America with the donut. When my grandfather needed to solve the problem of giving the machine users something to put in the machine, he went to see the first flour mill in this country, built in 1772 in Ellicott City, Maryland, where people had milled flour since before the American Revolution. He fell in love with this piece of America, dreamed of owning this flour mill. He rented a bit of the plant for his mix. The machine users bought this first fully prepared American mix, used it up, and needed more. Finally, he bought the mill.

Even when one day angry gusts of flame lashed at his beloved plant and ate the mill like a ravenous orange-and-black tiger loose from its pen, my grandfather bowed only briefly. His back straightened with purpose, with his freedom and his dream. He rebuilt the plant from the ground up.

In the machine shop of modern days, on the site of the original flour mill, a posse of elders in tweed suits, dressed up to show off, smelling of hair tonic, escorts me on a tour of machine parts, mammoths and dinosaurs of metal. They show them like prize pets. In a corner we see one of the first donut machines, a gleaming box, the so-called little machine. This one was used during the Depression by

THE DONUT MACHINE IN TIMES SQUARE

The *New Yorker* of July 1931 wrote:

We can tell you a little about the doughnut-making place in Broadway . . . Doughnuts float dreamily through a grease canal in a glass-enclosed machine, walk dreamily up a moving ramp, and tumble dreamily into an outgoing basket . . . The first time we stopped there the rail outside the window was heavy with people looking. A man whose straw hat moved when he chewed and a woman in a red dress were still there looking when we came back that way after more than half an hour. The man who invented the machine is a Mr. Adolph Levitt, who thought it up eleven years ago . . . Now he does a twenty-five million dollar business every year, selling the machines to bakers all over the world and selling them the makings, too.

small bakers, when breadlines became donut lines, and then it became obsolete. It stands as a memento. The company took back machines by the hundreds, scrapped them until a heap of parts from the little donut machines grew into a scrofulous rusted burial mound

DOUGHNUT CORPORATION OF AMERICA, big name in donut machines and donut mixes, built a towering business on an idea. Shell Industrial Lubricants played a big role in this phenomenal growth.

donuts to DOLLARS

DOLLARS TO DONUTS
Doughnut Corp. of America, a big name in donut machines and donut mixes, built a towering business on an idea.

in back of the plant. They tell me how years ago they all got jobs here in the Depression, outsmarting the breadlines and then staying because it was like home. These moguls of the machine shop, who have come together for the first time in 10 years to show me the plant, have 200 years of donut life in the company, which they call their "family." In fact, they called my grandfather, the Donut King, "Pop." They speak of him now as the "Father of Them All."

They speak of Pop with love. He was a despot but a benevolent one, Pop the Lion-hearted. He walked into the room and a hush fell over the men, like a silence after thunder. There was love in the hush.

The donut empire continued into the second generation, the mantle shifting to my father, whose name was David. After learning to work the donut machine his father had put in the basement for him to play with like pinball, he began, as a teenager, to trudge off to the bakery before dawn to collect donuts to put on top of milk bottles for people's breakfasts. Later, one summer, he made his way under an assumed name to the donut bakery in New York. No one was to know he was the Crown Prince. It was 105 degrees inside the bakery, where he worked for $10 a week. He learned to work the donut cutter incognito, until one day he set it wrong and miles of dough spilled all over the bakery. He had to give himself up so he wouldn't be fired.

After that my father became the Prince and the new Donut King, developing new donuts, like the jelly donut with a hole, and spreading donuts from Nigeria to Israel. He persuaded the U.S. government to let him dedicate the first donut machine in China. "Isn't it amazing," my father said, "that the son of the Russian village boy could bring donuts to China in the 1980s?" From the poor man's cake to the people's cake, a long journey.

When my grandfather stepped off the boat from Russia with his brothers and sisters, I think what they had in mind was survival, not

DUNKING STUNTS

The National Dunking Association had Hollywood stars as leaders and members. Dunking habits ran from dainty to surreptitious to aggressive, even destructive. Membership benefits included a card. If you were a contortionist, dunking stunts were easy.

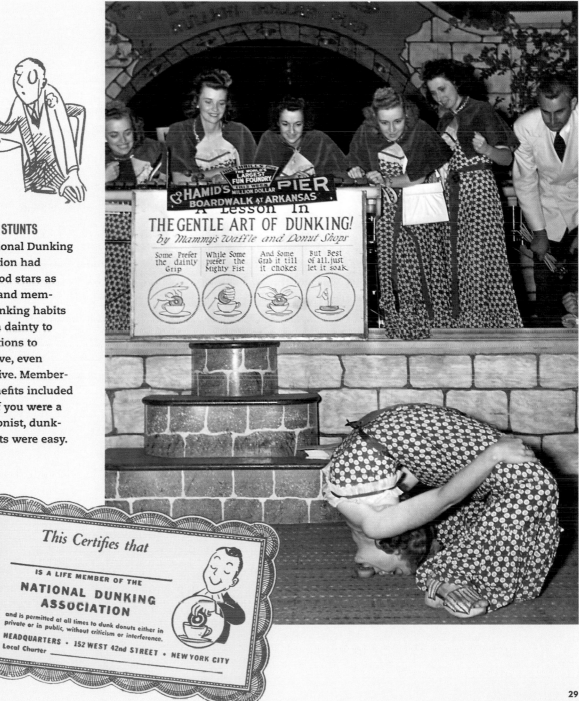

Cinnamon Sugar Donuts

Craft is one of New York's favorite temples of gastronomy. It is based on the concept of the highest-quality ingredients perfectly cooked and then "crafted" into a meal by the diner. This is one of pastry chef Karen Demasco's favorite recipes. *Makes about 15 donuts*

RAISED DONUTS

3½ cups bread flour
½ cup sugar
7 eggs
1 tablespoon plus 1½ teaspoons fresh yeast
1 tablespoon plus ¼ teaspoon kosher salt
1 pound unsalted butter, cold, plus more for greasing
Vegetable oil for frying

1. Combine the flour and sugar in an electric mixer with a dough hook. On medium speed, add the eggs one at a time. Mix until combined. Add the yeast. Next add the salt. When this comes together in a smooth ball around the hook, start adding the butter, piece by piece.

2. When the butter is fully incorporated, remove the dough from the mixer and place in a buttered bowl that is big enough for the dough to double. Cover and let proof.

3. When the dough has doubled in size, punch it down and refrigerate it overnight.

4. The next day, when the dough is thoroughly chilled, roll it out to about ¼ inch thick.

5. Cut into desired-size donuts, removing and reserving the holes (making donut holes is a must). Let them proof for 30 to 45 minutes, depending on how warm the room is. At this point, if they are too hard to handle, they can be rechilled for a short time.

6. Heat the oil to 390°F and fry the donuts, flipping them when they are golden. This should take about 2 minutes per side. Remove from the oil, drain on paper towels, and toss in Cinnamon Sugar.

CINNAMON SUGAR

1 pound superfine sugar
1 tablespoon ground cinnamon
½ teaspoon ground cardamom
¼ teaspoon salt

Combine all ingredients.

Some say donuts are life itself, an endless circle, repetitive, going nowhere, going everywhere and endlessly, eternal and ephemeral.

monarchy. But in making sure of his Americanness, he created something more American than he was, a machine to spread donuts all over the country so everyone could have one. He brought his brothers into the deal, Jake the peddler with the pushcart and John the storekeeper who kept going broke. They were gruff and solid; they were plain-spoken and bullish in their insistence on making it. My grandfather said, "If there were a better business, I'd be in it." They closed their determined jaws on cigars, clouded the air blue, turned it heavy to breathe, filled America with their dreams and their fists shaking at the sky.

So my grandfather took a common object, the donut, as lowly as his own start in life, and made it his own, gave it to America. He became the invisible spirit of coffee breaks and Halloween, living out his version of the American Dream.

Tim Hortons: Canadian Icon

Go anywhere in Canada and you're likely not far from a Tim Hortons, or two, or . . . Donuts are so popular in Canada that there are more donut shops per capita there than in any other country, including the U.S.

In 1964, Tim Horton, one of hockey's strongest defensemen, opened his first donut shop in Hamilton, Ontario. Horton died in a car accident in 1974, and in the years after his death, his partner, Ron Joyce, transformed a small regional chain into a Canadian icon by offering a place for people to meet, great donuts, and fresh, hot coffee — coffee so good that an urban legend has it that the chain adds nicotine to keep people coming back for more. There are now more than 2,300 Tim Hortons outlets across Canada and parts of the U.S.

Building on specialties Tim Horton, the man, developed, including dutchies (raisin-studded yeast donuts) and apple fritters, Tim Hortons, the shop, now offers soups and sandwiches. The Canadian giant has even intensified its expansion into the land of Dunkin' Donuts and Krispy Kreme with its conversion of 42 Bess Eaton stores in New England. Tim Hortons, Canadian classic, has become international.

NEW melt-in-your-mouth **toffee glazed**

Two

BELIEVE IT OR NOT

For purposes of identification, we need to know what we are talking about when we talk about donuts. Although the donut did not get its name until it came to America, the word *donut* is used to refer to fried sweet cakes everywhere and in all ages, with or without a hole. It is difficult to be exact, since people are not exact in their folklore and everyday speech. There have been many attempts at the definition of this elusive, multifaceted cake, which appears in so many guises that it seems to escape definition. *Donut* has become an umbrella term that includes crullers and fritters, twists and rings, round cakes and cakes filled with jelly and cream, donuts with holes and without, and even the holes themselves.

The *Oxford English Dictionary* and many other dictionaries say that a *doughnut* is a small cake sweetened and fried in oil, although the *World Book Dictionary* says a *doughnut* is "a circular tube in a betatron or synchratron that contains a vacuum in which electrons whirl and collide with the nuclei of the atoms in a small tungsten target to produce extremely powerful x-rays and gamma rays."

CENTER HOLE

Some people are purists, using the word *donut* to refer only to the ring-shaped cake with a hole that sprang into prominence in 19th-century America, when it got its hole and its name, the Great American Donut. A case that illustrates the nomenclature dispute is the classy import that accompanied the French a century ago to the city of New Orleans, the *beignet*, which you can still eat in the French market area of that city. Sprinkled with powdered sugar and eaten with chicory coffee, this little bit of fried matter with no hole is undeniably delicious. It is many people's choice for the best donut taste in this country. And yet, people ask, is it really a donut, and is it really an American donut? In French it is a beignet and also a *pet de nonne,* a nun's fart. We might call it a *deaunut,* which would Frenchify the name. Some folks say it cannot be American since it has the wrong "look." But even in American donut shops, all shapes qualify — stick and twist, ring and ball.

One conclusion might be this: A donut is a donut is a donut.

WHO'S WHO & WHAT'S WHAT OF DONUTS

My kids had a book of curious facts that says, on page two, "The average American eats two donuts a day." Donut-industry surveys say $2 billion worth of donuts are eaten in this country each year, 10 billion donuts. Nine out of 10 Americans eat donuts, says one authority. The one who doesn't is afraid of getting fat. Could all those pastries power a missile? Donuts are America's number one baked dessert, and in the baked goods market they are second only to bread.

Which means that almost everyone eats donuts. A veiled Kuwaiti woman and her two little boys, black bangs hanging over black eyes, eat donuts at an American school fair. Even my father, with his no-fat, no-flour, no-sugarn regime, ate donuts. How did he fit

THE BEST?
Some say beignets from the Café Du Monde in New Orleans are the best in America.

them in? "Well, once in a while," he would say, sipping a Coke and eating a donut between grain breakfasts and boiled vegetable dinners. FDR loved donuts. Admiral Richard Byrd took 100 barrels of donut flour, a two-year supply, to the glaciers of the Antarctic to warm his hands. President Reagan served them for breakfast.

People eat donuts for breakfast more than at any other time; snacktime comes in second. People are eating more donuts than ever. Some people think that donut-eating habits reflect the state of the economy. The worse the economy, the more people eat donuts, which goes back to that poor-man's-food idea. In 1929, the year of the Great Crash, U.S. residents ate 216 million donuts. Another reflector of the economy is the size of the hole. In hard times the hole gets bigger, because bakers are being frugal.

People eat them on ribbons of highways in the blazing sun. They warm their hands with donuts around a ski lodge fire or get up on the Ferris wheel over Coney Island, clutching them in the teetering seat. Prairie women made them for breakfast. Myra Waldo, food expert, says, "American women of an earlier era . . . had the art of frying donuts down pat. They had a good deal of practice, for the fried cakes were as much a breakfast staple as oatmeal porridge or bacon and eggs."

But donuts aren't just a lowbrow sweet. In 1903 the Isabella Stewart Gardner Museum

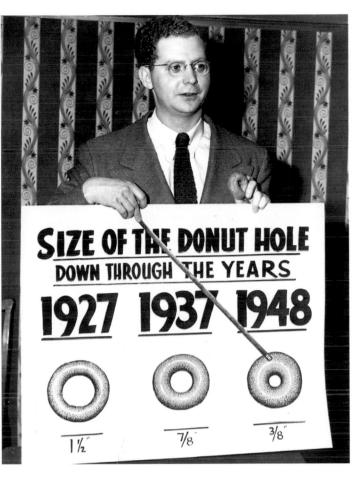

in Boston opened its ornate iron gates for the first time so the world could see its Venetian courtyard. Mrs. Gardner swept in with black pearls, the Boston Symphony played Bach and Mozart near the Roman mosaic and fountain in the candlelit courtyard, and guests drank champagne and ate donuts. Even Julia Child, apostle of French cooking, was known for her love of donuts. "I think good plain donuts are a lovely eatment," she said.

Economists say the size of the donut hole mirrors the state of the economy. In hard times, the hole gets bigger.

Hoppin' John Martin Taylor's Beignets

In New Orleans, beignets are square donuts without holes. They are sold every day at the old Café Du Monde in the French Quarter with big cups of café au lait. *Makes 16*

1 package active dry yeast
¼ cup warm water (110°F)
2 tablespoons granulated sugar
2 tablespoons unsalted butter
½ cup heavy (or whipping) cream
1 large egg
4 cups all-purpose flour
  Peanut oil for deep frying
  Confectioners' sugar for dusting

1. In a large bowl, dissolve the yeast in the warm water and allow to proof for about 10 minutes. It should become creamy and slightly bubbly.

2. Meanwhile, place the sugar, butter, and cream in a small saucepan and heat over low heat until the butter melts. Remove from the heat and allow to cool to lukewarm.

3. Beat the egg into the cream mixture. Then pour the mixture into the yeast and mix well. Add 2 cups of the flour and mix well, beating with a wooden spoon. Add another cup of flour and beat smooth again, then continue adding flour until the dough is no longer sticky. Add only as much flour as is necessary. Gather the dough into a ball and place it on a lightly floured work surface.

4. Pour oil to a depth of 3 inches in a Dutch oven or stockpot, place it over medium heat, and heat it to 365°F. Place a wire rack on a baking sheet and set it near the stove.

5. While the oil is heating, dust a rolling pin with flour and lightly roll out the dough, turning it a quarter turn, rolling it out some more, then turning it another quarter turn, until you have a 16-inch square about ¼ inch thick. Cut the dough into sixteen 4-inch squares.

6. When the oil reaches 365°F, lift up the squares with a spatula and drop two or three at a time into the oil. They will probably sink to the bottom of the pot. As soon as they rise to the surface (or when the underside is brown), turn them over and fry until crisp on the other side, about 3 minutes in all. Transfer them to the wire rack and continue frying the rest of the beignets, carefully maintaining the temperature between 360° and 370°F. Dust the drained beignets with confectioners' sugar and serve immediately.

WHAT'S IN A DONUT?

The Dutch donuts from 1673 made by Anna Joralemon, who ran the first donut shop in New York, and donuts made from machines and mixes today have the same basic combination of ingredients, give or take a few polysyllables. They are made of flour, sugar, shortening, leavening, egg, milk, and flavor. These ingredients were mixed by hand before the machine, and then these very same ingredients went into the original machines, along with loving care and the fervent hope that the end product would be a donut, which it sometimes was not. Occasionally shapeless masses of dough poured from the machine, and sometimes shapely but irregular objects resembling sea creatures or tropical plants emerged. My grandfather developed the first of the prepared mixes, granny to "box cakes," powders you stir and fry that end up donuts. The dough was mixed with a medium paddle and cooked at uniform temperature to emerge tender, not greasy, not tough. Now, of course, donuts, even Grandma's Old-Fashioned Donuts, have things like ammonium sulfate added for "shelf life." Other additives have made it into donuts by accident. Once a pigeon got into a machine and came out wrapped in dough. Doughbird. Once some muddy water from a river got into the dough and fouled it up. Locals referred to the result as Razorback Hog Juice Donuts.

Good donuts are delicate creatures depending on split-second timing. Ever since the machine was invented, experts have investigated how to get it just right. They studied how the dough rises, coagulates, holds gas, stretches. What pioneer women knew by touch has taken others years and dollars and sweat and study. For example, the amount of humidity on the skin of a rising donut can make or break the final product, so it needs a place to rise with the right temperature and humidity, which means the right part of the right

WHAT WAS THE BIGGEST DONUT EVER?
Some say that Anna Joralemon, the Dutch woman who ran a donut shop in the 17th century, will always be the biggest donut, since she weighed 225 pounds and was nicknamed "the Big Doughnut."

What kid can resist a donut?

Chocolate Donuts

This is one of the favorite donut recipes of Karen Demasco, Craft restaurant's talented pastry chef. *Makes about 15 donuts*

CHOCOLATE DONUTS

½ cup sugar

1½ teaspoons fresh yeast

½ cup warm water

1 pound bread flour, plus more for dusting

¾ cup cocoa powder

½ teaspoon salt

6 eggs

1 pound butter, cold

Vegetable oil for frying

1. In an electric mixer, whisk together the sugar, yeast, and water. Add the dry ingredients and mix with a dough hook until combined. Add the eggs all at once. Let this mix until the sticky dough comes together in a ball around the hook (about 10 minutes).

2. At this point, add the chilled butter in chunks and let it mix until the dough once again comes together around the hook.

3. Put it in an oiled bowl and let rise until doubled. Punch down the dough and chill for several hours or overnight.

4. On a floured surface, roll out the chilled dough to about ¾ inch. Cut into donuts, then let them proof for about 30 minutes.

5. While the dough is proofing, heat the oil to 390°F. Fry the donuts for about 2 minutes per side. Drain them on paper towels, then dip them into the Chocolate Glaze. Serve immediately.

These can be made ahead — cut and refrigerated (for one day) or frozen (for two weeks). When you are ready to use them, just thaw them out at room temperature and fry when they have begun to rise.

CHOCOLATE GLAZE

1 cup milk

2 cups confectioners' sugar

1 cup cocoa powder

4 tablespoons butter

In a saucepan, bring the milk to a boil. Pour it over the sugar and cocoa, then whisk in the butter. Strain.

... J. Howard Crum, M.D., consulting physician, Sun Diet Sanitarium, author of "Beauty and Health."

WHAT IS THE MOST OUTRAGEOUS FAD IN DONUTS?
Dr. Crum's famous Donut Reducing Diet, 1941.

...T WAY TO TAKE OFF POUNDS

Lost 10¼ pounds in 10 days
Donut diet has been a "pepper-up" besides reducing. I started on diet December 5th, my weight 144 lbs. on December 15th I weighed 133¾ lbs.
(name on request)

Easiest Diet to stay on
After 2 weeks of the donut diet I have lost 4 pounds . . . I find that the donut diet is the easiest to stay on that I have ever tried. I do not have the starved feeling I have had with previous diets.
(name on request)

No weakening effects
Enclosing weight tickets. Dec. 4 — 172¼ pounds . . . Dec. 20—168. I like this diet because it is very effective, not a starvation diet, has no weakening effect, is inexpensive, easily prepared.
(name on request)

...d
...uld
...gone
...e good
...rgy.
...m, made to
... they're di-
...ent is constant (im-
...g schedule). The Donut
...mon-sense way to take off pounds.

A copy of Dr. Crum's Donut Reducing Diet is waiting for you... FREE... at many food stores. Ask for it. Follow it out. You'll say it's one of the most pleasant and sensible reducing diets ever.

GET YOUR FREE
"DONUT DIET" LEAFLET
WHERE YOU SEE THIS SIGN →

Now **FREE!**
Dr. Howard Crum's
"DONUT REDUCING DIET"
with every purchase of
DONUTS

LOOK FOR THIS SEAL →

★ *Different* ★ *Delicious* ★ *Digestible* ★ *Doughnuts*

DOUGHNUT CORP. OF AMERICA, NEW YORK CITY

... J. Howard Crum, M.D., consulting physician, Sun Diet Sanitarium, author of "Beauty and Health."

machine with the right amount of air at the right moment. A donut takes just 14 minutes to mix, needs 120 degrees to make a skin, and spends 85 seconds in the fryer. It gets a poke test and a crease test. It takes 55 minutes from mix to ready to eat.

Looked at another way, donuts have 15 to 25 percent fat, so junk food expert Michael S.

Lasky says, "Donuts cannot be eaten without compensatory action in the rest of the diet." Cake donuts have 15 percent sugar; yeast-raised, only 3 percent. Plain donuts have 200 to 250 calories; topped, filled, or frosted donuts have 400 to 500. The plain one equals a slice of bread with butter and jam.

What's in a donut? Heaven and earth, life and death, a moment of sweetness, a moment of indulgence, a moment of guilt, a moment of union with the other thousands who at this very moment, somewhere on earth, are also eating donuts.

WHAT KINDS ARE THERE?

Donuts come in a variety as great as that of Americans, almost. If you are a donut maker, you find out quickly that, even in a machine, no two donuts are ever alike, just like people. They defy uniformity. There are variations of shape and texture — a bulge here, a dent there. There are toppings, icings, fillings, and flavors. If you multiply all this variety, you get thousands of possibilities. A mix plant has more than 400 mixes. Even the package differs widely, with yellow as the most popular color for donut packages, black the least.

Donuts have distinct personalities. A Long John is an oblong, yeast-raised donut. A Hole-in-One is a donut with ice cream and fudge. Donut holes, poked from the middle and fried up, are called Munchkins, Smidgets, PopEms.

WHO'S WHO:

Glazed

Jelly

Zebra stripes

Confetti sprinkles

Coconut

Chocolate frosted

Vanilla frosted

There are molasses donuts (are the holes called Slow Pokes?), maple donuts, pumpkin donuts, peanut butter donuts, even bacon-and-egg donuts. There are cider mill and Boston cream, butter crunch and buttermilk donuts. Dunkerettes are half-donuts for dunking. There are grapefruit peel donuts and fruitcake donuts and malted milk donuts and honey bran donuts. There are donuts topped with marshmallow or meringue, ones filled with marmalade and fig. There are "lite" donuts for weight watchers.

WHICH ARE BEST?

For popularity by numbers, the yeast-raised, honey-dipped (glazed) wins even over chocolate. But real donut lovers know that back on the farm, Grandma knew more about split-second timing to get a donut that "eats well." Some real American donut lovers say that the beignet, the French market donuts from New Orleans, which are among the "original donuts" in this country, are best.

The most important donut in your life or anyone else's is probably not your first donut but your best. A consumer research group once did a statistical survey of eating out and found that pizza has romance, so people remember their first pizza like their first kiss. But donuts blur, because we eat so many at different times, except for that absolutely best donut ever.

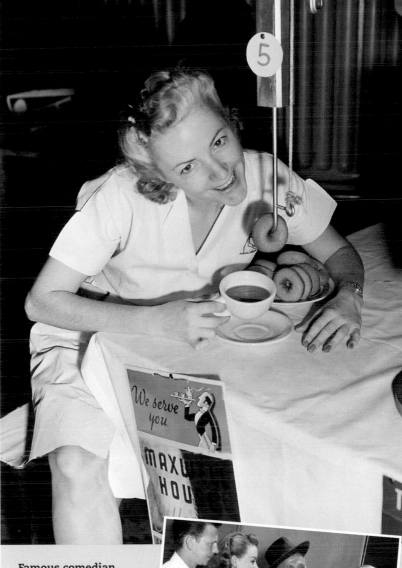

Famous comedian Jimmy Durante had a donut-dunking routine. Is that why he was a candidate for president of the National Dunking Association (right)? Others take the lazy way out (above).

Rose petals on the rosewater doughnut from the Doughnut Plant in New York City.

WHO DUNKS DONUTS?

"That's how the donut crumbles," said Zero Mostel after dunking a donut in *A Funny Thing Happened on the Way to the Forum* (below). America's most famous Donut Hole, California (right).

Most everyone, and it's easy when you have a donut with a handle, like the one made by Dunkin' Donuts. Jimmy Durante had a donut-dunking routine. Adlai Stevenson dunked donuts gingerly, and Eisenhower dunked them during and after the war.

Some say the first to dunk were Baptists called the Dunkards. Others say the trend began when Civil War soldiers dunked hardtack in coffee. Still others say the actress Mae Murray invented it at Lindy's when she accidentally dropped her donut in coffee, and her escort followed suit to keep her company.

The most spectacular dunking was performed by Shipwreck Kelly, the famous stuntman and flagpole sitter. He was able to dunk 13 donuts while standing on his head on a plank extended from a New York skyscraper on Friday the 13th.

WHAT IS THE MOST FAMOUS DONUT?

It might be the donut featured on the TV program *Evening Magazine,* or the ones eaten by presidential candidates Carter and Reagan from the same donut shop before their debate.

It might be the huge donut made for Zero Mostel in 1962, when he starred in *A Funny Thing Happened on the Way to the Forum.* He was judged by the Donut Institute "the man most likely to succeed in keeping his toga dry while dunking." His comment on the honor: *"Sic crustulum friat,"* or, translated from the Latin, "That's how the donut crumbles."

It might be one of the donuts President Clinton sent out for in the middle of the night when he felt the "call."

It might be that most-longed-for donut, the Chock Full O'Nuts Whole Wheat Donut from the 1960s, which is everybody's favorite and is coming back.

It might be Mark Isreal's pistachio and rose petal donut made with all organic ingredients at his Doughnut Plant in New York.

It might be the donut at Dunkin' Donuts, which has the greatest number of shops in the world. There are shops even in the Philippines. And it might be, and probably is,

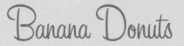

Banana Donuts

Light, tender, and full of cinnamon sugar, these donuts are packed with wonderful flavors. Adapted from *Nicole Routhier's Fruit Cookbook*. *Makes 16 donuts*

2¾ cups unbleached, all-purpose flour

1½ teaspoons baking powder

1 teaspoon baking soda

3 teaspoons ground cinnamon

3 tablespoons unsalted butter

1½ cups plus 2 tablespoons sugar

2 large eggs

¼ cup milk

¼ cup orange, pineapple, or apple juice

1 teaspoon vanilla extract

2 medium, ripe bananas, diced into ¼-inch cubes

Vegetable oil for deep frying

1. Sift together the flour, baking powder, baking soda, and 1 teaspoon of the cinnamon into a large bowl. Make a well in the center.

2. Cream the butter and ½ cup plus 2 tablespoons of the sugar in a small bowl. Beat in the eggs. Stir in the milk, fruit juice, vanilla, and bananas. Pour this mixture into the center of the dry ingredients and stir with a wooden spoon just until blended. The dough should be very soft but not sticky. Do not overmix.

3. Cover and chill the dough for 1 hour.

4. Place half of the dough on a well-floured board, knead lightly, and pat it into a circle approximately ¾ inch thick. Cut with a floured 2½-inch donut cutter. Gather the dough scraps, knead briefly, and pat into a ¾-inch-thick circle, and cut out more donuts. Continue until all the dough is used up. Place the donuts on a lightly floured baking sheet while you work with the remaining half of the dough.

5. Pour oil to a depth of 2 inches into a large, heavy skillet (if using a deep-fryer, add oil to a depth of 3½ inches). Slowly heat the oil to 350°F over medium heat. Fry the donuts, in batches, until golden brown on both sides, about 2 minutes. Do not overcrowd the skillet. Drain on paper towels. Keep warm in a low oven as you fry the remaining donuts. Be sure the oil returns to 350°F before you fry the next batch.

6. Mix the remaining 1 cup of sugar and the remaining 2 teaspoons of cinnamon in a medium-size bowl. Roll the warm donuts in the sugar mixture and serve at once.

the Krispy Kreme donut in all its variety, which has conquered the country and is aiming to conquer the world.

WHAT IS THE MOST FAMOUS DONUT HOLE?

La Puente, California, hosts the famous Donut Hole, a donut-shaped shop with a road called Donut Lane going through its center. Customers drive through the hole to order sweets. In 1984 the Donut Hole was featured on the TV program *Smithsonian World*, in a segment called "Speaking without Words." The shop calls out to people along the road, a sort of show-and-tell to the crowds. The narrator of the program said, "There's a donut you can dunk into." The owner of the Donut Hole said, "They call it the Hole. About two years ago one of the newspapers put us down, called us a car wash, a drive-through car wash. Didn't bother me, really didn't. People come over to take pictures. I think it's because it's so unusual. People get to drive through. They don't ever have to get out of the car."

MARES MAY EAT OATS, BUT BEARS EAT DONUTS

We all know that people eat donuts, but I wonder how many people know that bears like donuts even more than marshmallows dipped in syrup or suet smeared with molasses. John McPhee reports on the bears of New Jersey, that state where the turnpike offers up a surrealistic grid of hellfire-and-damnation towers and power plants and factories intricately webbed, with crisscrossing networks of pipelines and funnels and fuel towers topped with the flames of burning chemicals. Just down the road a bit are the Pine Barrens, forests untouched by human construction, great pine trees giving shade, shedding needles for chipmunk beds. Among the groves are roaming bears and the trapper who lures them to her lair. Thanks mostly to one object, the donut, she has been able to observe the state's bears consistently.

The trapper puts donuts into her metal-cage trap and then makes a trail of donuts leading off into the woods. "A bear that comes along eating Dutch Apple and Sugar-Raised goes on . . . and grabs the fishnet bag, which is attached to a wire that runs back along the top of the barrel and releases the Damoclean door." When the trapper strews donuts around, they always disappear "to the last cruller." The nearby Dunkin' Donuts franchise has pictures of bears all over it. "Every bear we have caught this year we have caught on Dunkin' Donuts . . . Crullers, lemon-filled, cream-filled, jelly . . . The bears have been climbing in and out for Dunkin' Donuts." The lady bears are smart, though. Sometimes they eat the donuts but escape the trap.

Bears have lots of fat. After eating all those donuts, they sleep almost all winter, eating practically nothing and still waking up with two thirds of their fat untouched. It is partly the donuts that make this bear fat. Bear fat in early American times was highly recommended for the cooking of donuts — a sort of coals-to-Newcastle situation.

NUN'S FARTS?

A common French word for the sweet fried cake, the beignet, is *pet de nonne*, which means "nun's fart." This translation of *donut* even traveled to England, where, in Elizabethan times, the word *fartes* meant "balls of light pastry, also known as puffs," according to J. Favre in *Dictionnaire de la Cuisine*.

In the ancient abbey of Marmoutier lived a young and beautiful novice nun, Agnes. On the feast day of Saint Martin, she was occupied in helping the abbess, renowned for her culinary talents, in the gastronomic preparations of the day. Agnes listened to the instructions of the abbess, while playing absently with a ball of raw dough on a spoon over a pot of boiling oil. A strange noise, loud and long, like the trembling of an organ or the breeze sighing in the cloisters, struck the ears of the good nuns, rousing them from their activities. Did it come from the devil? *Mais non!* It issued from beneath the robe of Agnes, the petite, lily-white nun. Instantly pink angels

DONUTS FROM OUR PAST

Pet de Nonne

½ litre d'eau (½ liter water)
400 g de farine (400 grams flour)
200 g de beurre (200 grams butter)
12 à 15 oeufs entiers (12 to 15 whole eggs)
2 zestes de citrons (zest of 2 lemons)
2 g baking powder (2 grams baking powder)
1 pincée de sel (1 pinch of salt)
1 pincée de sucre (1 pinch of sugar)
2 cuillères d'eau de fleurs d'oranger
    (2 tablespoons orange flower water)

2 fritures: 1 tié pour demarrer (2 fryings: 1 lukewarm).
Cuire au four (Cook in oven).
Retremper dans friture chaude pour colorer si besoin est. Pas besoin si beignets bien faits (Rewarm in hot fat if necessary to brown).
Cuire à friteuse assez chaude pour empêcher les beignets de pomper l'huile (Cook in hot fat).

EQUIVALENCIES

1 liter = 4 cups = 1 quart (or ½ liter = 2 cups = 1 pint)
400 grams = 14 ounces
200 grams = about 7 ounces
2 grams = less than 1 ounce

arose to stifle the noise, hiding giggles behind their white wings. But, alas, it was already too loud. Agnes, beneath the severe gaze of the elder nuns, became as white as wax, then redder than a wild strawberry, and let fall from her spoon the nugget of dough into the hot oil.

Oh, miracle! The dough swelled. It became round, a golden globe. The women gathered around, marveled, tasted. What a wonder! A new and incomparable sweet delectable had been discovered. They called it *Pet de Nonne*, Nun's Fart, in memory of Agnes.

DO DONUTS HAVE ANY PROBLEMS?

Mrs. Donut, round and always smiling.

Absolutely. Wouldn't you if your body had to relax and then shrink, if you needed a poke test, a crease test, even a membrane test? One troubleshooting chart shows that the problems donuts have are a lot like ours. Blisters, sour taste, overweight, too dark, collapsed — sounds like me at the end of the day. Therapy may require a minute change in the rate gas escapes from dough, or an extensograph to measure how dough stretches, or a farinograph to get the consistency right. One batch of yeast-raised donuts in a factory suddenly decided not to rise. After prolonged puzzlement, another well was chosen for the water in the dough. So

in spite of its hale and hearty image, the donut is capable of trauma from a subtle shift of time, temperature, or ingredients. In the trade, a well-adjusted donut is known as an "educated donut," with "ease of bite."

Even the machine has had problems. If there are too many vibrations in the sugaring operation, crumbs result, not donuts. A second of too little heat in the box where donuts rise, and they stick to the tray.

Then, of course, there are the image problems everyone knows about. The donut is too common, too lowly, too greasy, too fattening, too indigestible, too junk food. In spite of all these difficulties, though, the donut has survived from prairie breakfast to around-the-clock snack.

WHAT CAN DONUTS DO?

Donuts can have problems and they can create them. On the highway I saw a man stuff a chocolate donut into his mouth. Then his car skidded into two other cars for a three-car crack-up.

With the coming of the donut, the coffee break reached its potential as a ritual retreat from desks and typewriters and assembly lines and computers. Biologists who study our rhythms say we work in cycles of an hour and a half; that's as much attention as we have before we need a break, sometimes with a snack. Donuts punctuate our body rhythms.

Shipwreck Kelly dunks 13 donuts on Friday the 13th.

WHAT ARE THE FIRSTS IN DONUTS?

The world's first donut was yeast-raised, like bread. Before the first donut machine, donuts were made either by hand in a frying pan or with a hand crank over a pot of oil. The first donut company was the Doughnut Corporation of America. The first retail donut shop was in Times Square in 1931, the Mayflower Shop, later to become one of America's first chains. The first package of donuts was the "bag pack," six donuts wrapped in wax paper. Many people ate their first donut at the World's Fair in 1933, where "modern" donut production by automatic machine was on display for the first time to millions. The first device to produce a donut with a hole was the donut cutter, invented by John Blondel in 1872 in Maine. It was a spring cutter with a center tube. The first American promotion for a food product was Donut Month, October 1929.

DOUGHBOYS AND DONUTS

Did doughboys get their name from donuts? The answer lies buried in the archives of American slang, which has been rolling in dough for a long time. There are also dough-faces and doughheads; the word *donut* can even refer to human types like idiots or dupes. *Doughface* is unrelated to donuts. It means a northerner who supported slavery during the Civil War. It came to mean weak willed. A doughhead is a fool or dumb person.

A *doughgirl*, otherwise known as Doughnut Girl or Doughnut Dolly or Sally, is a term for a woman who made donuts in World Wars I and II. The name *doughboy* is popularly thought to mean soldiers who eat donuts. Even Stella Young, the original Doughnut Girl from World War I, still thought so in the 1980s. This trend continued into World War II, and the term became part of American slang.

Although this explanation for the origin of doughboy is widespread, it is a misconcep-

DONUTS FROM OUR PAST

Doughboys

This recipe is from the *Fannie Farmer Boston Cooking School Cookbook.*

Roll bread dough to ⅛ inch thick. Cut in strips 2½ inches wide and cut the strips in squares or in diamond-shaped pieces. Cover and let stand 10 to 15 minutes. Fry like doughnuts. Serve in place of hot rolls or with maple syrup as a breakfast dish or as a dessert.

there. Yet another story says that in the 1850s, soldiers in Texas cleaned their belts with dough made of clay and so were called doughboys. In 1809 in Spain, British soldiers were called doughboys because they made dough from grain during a food shortage. A later variant of the doughboy appears on the packages of Pillsbury flours and mixes.

LORD OF THE RINGS: HOW BAGELS AND DONUTS ARE RELATED

tion. The word originated long before donuts and soldiers got together, when doughboys were not always people but food. The *Oxford English Dictionary* says that a doughboy is "a boiled flour dumpling." The first reference goes as far back as 1685: "These men . . . had each of them three or four Cakes of bread (called by the English Dough-Boy's) for their provision and Victuals." In America the original doughboy dumpling was popular with soldiers. It was often served aboard ship with hash. One explanation for the origin of the word is that the soldiers of the Civil War had buttons on their uniforms that looked like dumplings, so the men were called doughboys. Another story says the word *doughboy* came from "dobie boy," in the mid-19th century, originating with the word *adobe*, because the uniforms of the southwestern American soldiers looked like the dusty adobe used in buildings

No discussion of the donut would be complete without facing up to the bagel issue — the mutual influence of those lookalikes, their different upbringings, and their shared tendency to cause weight gain. It seems unfair to this pair of associates to talk about one without the other, especially since they have lived in harmony over the centuries.

The bagel has been called a "donut gone astray," a "cement" or "petrified" donut, and a "donut with a Jewish education." Similarly, a donut

Soldiers and donuts have always been companions.

Buttermilk Donuts

This comes from *American Food,* by Evan Jones.

Makes about 16

    2 eggs
    1 egg yolk
    1 cup sugar
    1 cup buttermilk
    4 cups all-purpose flour
    1 teaspoon baking powder
    ¼ teaspoon baking soda
    ½ teaspoon salt
    ½ teaspoon freshly grated nutmeg
    1 tablespoon butter, melted
       Oil for deep frying

1. Beat eggs and yolk together, then gradually add sugar and buttermilk. Sift flour, baking powder, baking soda, and salt together and stir into egg mixture; add nutmeg and melted butter.

2. Heat oil to 360°F.

3. Roll or pat dough on a floured surface to ½-inch thickness.

4. Drop donuts, a few at a time, into hot oil. Fry until golden brown (2 to 3 minutes).

5. Drain on paper towels and serve immediately.

has been called a "Gentile bagel." The modern-day donut is American, whereas the bagel is an immigrant. On the one hand, the bagel's foreign beginnings make it seem more exotic than the lowly donut, the poor man's rich food. On the other hand, the donut wins for the venerability of its pedigree. Its origins at the dawn of civilized humans (round pastries appear in ancient records) give it credentials that the bagel, the newly arrived creature of East European cities, lacks.

What makes a bagel a bagel is that the dough is boiled and then baked, giving it a distinctive texture. Donut and bagel alike are accused of heaviness, but the bagel gets away with it by not being sweet, which makes it seem more virtuous. However, its rubbery properties add pounds, especially when slathered with cream cheese and topped with lox. Both bagel and donut have been thought to appeal to the poor, as the hole saves money. One old Yiddish bagel recipe explains that you take a hole and put some dough around it.

As with stories of the origins of donuts, the tales of the beginnings of bagels and their Jewishness are not based on hard facts. One source traces the first use of the word *bagel* to the Community Regulations of Cracow in 1610, as an item given to women in childbirth. The most common story dates from a bit later in the same century. In 1683 the king of Poland freed the Austrians from Turkish attack, so the grateful Austrians grabbed the

THE DONUT DIP
FRESH BAGELS

king's stirrups on his victory ride through Vienna. Next a Viennese baker had the bright idea of making a bread shaped like a stirrup in commemoration of the victory, naming it *Bügel*, the German word meaning stirrup or bow. The connection between Jews and bagels is hazy in its origins but firm in its reality. The bread's journey to America seems to have coincided with the arrival of Jews from Austria and Germany, but by now it has gone full "circle" and is eaten by American Jew and non-Jew alike. In fact, one of the biggest Bagel Days in America is St. Patrick's Day, when green bagels appear on the streets, an extreme in culture mix. On a much publicized occasion, Teddy Kollek, mayor of Jerusalem, wore clerical robes at the Cathedral of St. John the Divine in New York. After the ceremony the dean of the church invited the congregation to a reception with loaves and fishes, otherwise known as bagels and lox.

Like the donut, the bagel has been used to symbolize the continuous circle of life and death, and so it was connected to various holidays for luck. Its presentation to women in childbirth was an example of this, and it was eaten at funerals to represent life everlasting. By contrast, in one old Yiddish expression, the meaning of the bagel is not so salutary. "May he lie in the earth and bake bagels" means "May he drop dead." So both the donut and the bagel represent that universal, eternal, perfect form, symbolic of life and death, of good luck and bad.

ON NAMES AND NOMENCLATURE

What's in a name? Would a donut by any other name smell as sweet? What if, instead of "donuts," donuts were called "thoughts"? Or "moons?" or "myths"? Have a moon for dessert. Would you like milk with your thought? Do you like myths with holes? I would like a chocolate moon and a frosted myth. Do you like raised thoughts? Did you finish your moon with sprinkles? Myths are really good filled with ice cream. I always take moons to baseball games. There is usually time for sugared thoughts at the beach. Does your mother like jelly moons? What is your favorite thought? Who put the hole in the moon? Is it a moon without its hole?

Three

WHODUNIT, WHODONUT

Once upon a time there were no donuts peeking out of the windows of boxes with "Reg. Penna. Dept. Agr." on the side. Fried cakes, or donuts, first without the holes and then later through the ages with holes and without, have been around since fat and flour have existed, the oldest ancestors of our coffee-break staple. The Bible says someone once fried a cake and it was good.

Who done the donut first? We all did, even though people think it is an American invention. Those who were around in early Fertile Crescent days found out about grinding grain into flour, mixing the flour with water to make dough, frying it in oil, and pouring honey over it. In this way, the first sweet fried cake was born, one of humanity's oldest and simplest foods, the original desert dessert. All you needed was a cooking vessel or pot and a fire to heat it, which was the most primitive cooking technology, easier than an oven, which needed long firing. The discussion of the laws of sacrifice in Leviticus 7:12 says that "cakes mingled with oil . . . of fine flour, fried" should be used as thanksgiving offerings to God.

Down through the ages all societies had some form of this food, the simple fried cake, to be tossed in the air for luck at Christmastime, to symbolize the cycle of life and death at funerals. The cakes were sweetened with rose water or honey and studded with nuts or dried fruits. They were twirled into circles in Spain and twisted into knots in northern Europe. It is even told that a fried cake with a hole was found petrified under the lava at Pompeii.

Sweet fried cakes, called by the name fritters, appear in very early cooking texts all over the world, from the Orient to the Middle East to medieval Europe, from the "hot and smoking deep of time itself," in the words of Robert Courtine, food expert. Later they got their national names — churros, olykoeks, dumplings, ciambelli, fasnachts, beignets, crullers, and, yes, donuts. Courtine writes, "Holidays . . . all have their fritter to buttress them, the traditional ritual of folklore . . . every village has its fritter."

The *Middle English Dictionary* contains a recipe for the "friture" from 1381. It says, "[M]ake therto a batour" with "flowre" and "fry hem wyth fresch grees."

Another medieval manuscript has one for "Oreoles, or Elderberry Funnel Cakes," in which batter is piped through a tube and fried in oil in "spiral or any imaginative shapes." The *Proper Newe Book of Cokerye* contains a 16th-century recipe for "frytures" of spice, egg, and flour fried in suet and shaped into "pilles as big as a walnut."

The other medieval ancestor of the donut is the jumble, which still exists as either a baked or a fried cake, sometimes more of a cookie than a donut, but with the distinction of having the ring shape we think Americans invented for donuts in the 19th century. This medieval dessert was either circular or, less frequently, looped to make two holes. The word *jumble,* which appeared in the 1600s, derives from *Gimmel* or *Gimble* or *cymbal,* all of which meant finger ring. Much later, in the 20th century, there appeared a colloquial word for donuts, *cymbals,* which probably came from this root.

THE DONUT FAMILY TREE

After these early versions of the fried cake, this popular sweet proliferated, emerging in different shapes with different names and with differing tastes and customs and rituals of consumption. There is little logic to this topsy-turvy growth of donuts and their cousins and uncles and aunts. To make matters worse, there are misnomers and popular misconcep-

ALL SHAPES & SIZES
Round donuts with holes are the "American" donut shape. But donuts can be twisted or oblong or tied into knots, or even round without holes.

tions. For example, people think the donut with a hole was invented by a whaling captain in America, and the captain himself thought so too. But the fact is that the holey donut has been around for centuries in Europe. To trace the evolution of this variegated species, we have to use not a logical system but an impressionistic one, keeping track of shape and name and taste and ritual all at once.

All societies had dumplings and fried doughs, sweetened and unsweetened lookalikes, some made with yeast and some not. There were fried breads and pretzels and bagels and johnnycakes and pancakes, all of which were related to donuts in shape or texture or taste, but which may have taken another route on the evolutionary highway.

A good example of this mix-up is the cruller/pretzel/donut/bagel axis. The pretzel is to the cruller what the bagel is to the donut, an unsweetened, unfried lookalike relative. As for the bagel and the donut, the round shape for bread and baked goods was a common one, with its variations of size, height, or elongation. There was also the twist, which gave rise to an interesting invention, the pretzel. Lore says that the pretzel was accidentally born when bread dough was overbaked in a fourth-century monastery kitchen. The shape has a variety of explanations. One is that it represented angels with arms crossed in prayer or supplication. Another is that it came from a game where man is pulled between

Elderberry Funnel Cakes

This is from a medieval manuscript, a recipe still made by the American Pennsylvania Dutch. The batter is piped through a tube into "amusing or fantastic shapes." From *Madeleine Cosman, Fabulous Feasts: Medieval Cookery and Ceremony*, 1976.

- ½ teaspoon salt
- 2 eggs, beaten
- 2 cups milk
- 2 cups flour
- 1 scant teaspoon baking powder
- ½ cup elderberry or plum preserves
  Funnel or pastry tube
- 1–2 cups oil for frying
  Honey

Add salt to eggs and stir both into milk. Sift flour with baking powder. Mix milk and eggs with flour. Add preserves to mixture, and add more milk or flour to make batter thick enough to pipe through tube. Into hot oil pipe batter in "spiral or any imaginative shapes, making initials or designs." Fry until golden, drain, then drizzle with honey.

These fried strips are one kind of *churro*, a Spanish donut sometimes tied into a ring by *churreras*, women who make and sell them on the street.

God and the devil. The cruller has the same figure-eight or twisted shape, and it's anybody's guess what it means. Another suggestion is that it was a variation of the ring shape, which was originally a serpent, symbol of the cycle of life, twisted around a stick, once for the ring, twice for the twist. Still another theory holds that the shape depicted a knot, the lover's knot, which tied lovers together. A footnote to this is that one name given to donuts of all shapes later in history was "twister."

In 1943, L. H. Robbins of the *New York Times* wrote an article called "Doughnut or Cruller?" that gave rise to an avalanche of mail about what donuts are. He cited disputes between grandmothers (who said that donuts are yeast-raised cakes and crullers are leavened with baking powder) and the Dunking Association (which called a cruller a twisted cake and a donut a round cake with a

hole). Then he said that most people call all these things a donut. Robbins's final word: "Interest in the donut appears to be immense, even in parlous times like these."

From the Fertile Crescent and from medieval manuscripts, donuts made their way all over the world. In northern Europe they were especially part of Shrove Tuesday. People in other countries ate them on Christmas or New Year's or All Saints' Day. Some people think the five gold rings in the Christmas songs are donuts. In Germany jelly

DONUTS FROM OUR PAST

Doughnuts

From Mrs. Ellis's Housekeeping Made Easy, or Complete Instructor in All Branches of Cookery and Domestic Economy, containing the most modern and approved receipts of daily service in all families. Revised and adapted to the Wants of the Ladies of the United States, 1943.

Combine 1½ pounds flour, 3 eggs, ½ spoonful pearl ash [potassium carbonate], 2 ounces butter, 6 ounces sugar, and 1 cup milk. Spice to your taste and fry in lard.

donuts, or *Pfannkuchen*, brought good luck when eaten after midnight on New Year's. In Holland the fried cakes were part of the celebration of Saint Nicholas Day.

There is also a venerable Celtic tradition in Great Britain of eating fried cakes on All Hallows' Eve. In pagan England's misty glens, the Celts gave fried cakes as a charity offering to widows and orphans on October 31, the day before winter, perhaps to protect them from the cold by laying down an ounce of flesh.

Italians have donuts called *zeppole* or *ciambelli*, which, among other things, means tire. Hungarians have donuts filled with prune butter. The Danish have *aebleskiver*, which are made in the dimples of a round copper pan and turned with a knitting needle. The Greeks eat *loukoumades*, a sweet fritter dipped in honey, one of the oldest known fried cakes. They were originally wheat cakes fried on an iron griddle and covered with grape molasses. In Israel donuts called *sufganiyot* are a Hanukkah specialty, and Indian Jews have their own version, *bimuelos*, which they eat instead of potato pancakes. Other Indians have a kind of donut called *jaleki*, made with saffron and corn syrup. Even the Chinese have an indigenous donutlike cake, a rice-flour pastry covered with sesame seeds and filled with sweetened bean paste.

In Spain the fried cake has been part of everyday life for centuries. The Spanish were one of the first nationalities to develop the fried cake with a hole, not just as a holiday treat but as a daily snack. Early Spanish documents contain abundant evidence of donuts. Even in the 17th century, Cervantes mentions them in *Don Quixote*. In the first Spanish cookbook, by Rupert de Nola in 1525,

Harvest Time is DONUT TIME

1949 • 21ST Annual OCTOBER DONUT MONTH

Loukoumades

Greek donuts, or *loukoumades,* are associated with many holidays and rituals. Mastic is a flavorful Greek tree resin that is sold in Middle Eastern shops. The fritters are often covered in sticky sweet syrup and piled into a tower shape. *Makes about 80 loukoumades.*

3	tablespoons dry yeast
2½	cups warm water
1	tablespoon mastic
2	tablespoons sugar
6	cups all-purpose flour, plus ½ cup
1	teaspoon sea salt
1	egg, slightly beaten
2½	cups milk
6	tablespoons ouzo
	Oil for frying

1. Dissolve the yeast in a small bowl with the warm water. Let sit 10 minutes.

2. Meanwhile, grind the mastic and sugar together and add to 6 cups of the flour and the salt. Sift these ingredients together over a piece of parchment paper and pour them all into a large stainless-steel bowl.

3. Make a well in the dry ingredients and add the beaten egg.

4. Pour the milk and the ouzo into the dissolved yeast mixture once 10 minutes have passed, and mix well. Pour this liquid into the well in stages and, using a heavy wire whisk, mix the wet into the dry. Mix evenly to distribute but do not overmix. The batter should be thick but pourable. Cover with plastic wrap and let sit 1½ hours, until double in size. If too wet, add the last ½ cup of flour.

5. Heat 3 to 4 inches of oil to 360°F in a deep, heavy saucepan.

6. Drop tablespoons of batter into hot oil. Cook, turning occasionally, until balls are golden brown. Remove from oil and drain on paper towels. Serve immediately.

LOUKOMADES

- 6-6½ cups   A.P. FLOUR
- 3 T   DRY YEAST
- 2½ C   WARM WATER
- 2½ C   MILK
- 1 tsp   SEA SALT
- 1 T   MASTIC
- 2 T   SUGAR
- 6 T   OUZO
- 1 eg   EGG, SLIGHTLY BEATEN

DISSOLVE THE YEAST IN A SMALL BOWL WITH THE WARM WATER; LET SIT 10 MINUTES. GRIND THE MASTIC AND THE SUGAR TOGETHER AND ADD TO THE FLOUR AND SALT. SIFT ALL THE DRY INGREDIENTS TOGETHER OVER A PIECE OF PARCHMENT PAPER, THEN POUR ALL THE DRY INGREDIENTS INTO A LARGE STAINLESS STEEL BOWL. MAKE A WELL IN THE BOTTOM CENTER OF THE BOWL AND ADD THE BEATEN EGG. POUR THE MILK + THE OUZO INTO THE DISSOLVED YEAST MIXTURE (IF 10 MINUTES HAS PASSED) AND MIX WELL. POUR THE LIQUID INTO THE WELL (IN STAGES) AND USING A HEAVY WIRE WHIP, MIX THE WET INTO THE DRY WITH THE DRY BECOMES WET. MIX EVENLY TO DISTRIBUTE BUT DO NOT OVERMIX. THE BATTER SHOULD BE THICK BUT POURABLE. COVER W/PLASTIC WRAP AND LET SIT ABOUT 1½ HRS, DOUBLE IN SIZE.

there is a recipe for *rosquillas*, which translates as "ring-shaped fritter" or "donut." Some say these cakes originated in Morocco with the Moors. There is also an early Spanish recipe for a donutlike cake called *buñuelos de viento*, or "puffs of wind," which were eaten on All Saints' Day, when the Spanish pay respect to the dead by visiting their burial sites. In the 17th century, 1627 to be exact, there was visual proof of the existence of the Spanish donut-with-hole in a painting by Juan Hamen y Leon. It pictures food and household objects, and there, big as life, is a sugared donut with a hole just like the ones in the corner shop. *Still Life with Donut*, I call it.

Continuing in this ancient tradition, the streets of Spain today are full of *churreras*, women vendors in colorful clothes who have been frying the ring-shaped cake called the *churro* for centuries. The women make the dough at home and fry it on the street in a kettle of oil with a burner at the bottom. They take strips of dough and join them at the ends to make a circle, or they pass the dough through a special tube of metal made for these cakes, a bit like the American donut cutter. Then they thread them on reeds. These churreras serve the Spanish populace this snack at breakfast or teatime or very late at night. People also dunk them in hot chocolate, especially if they indulge in the custom of churro eating at 4 A.M., after a night of flamenco music. The Churreria de San Gines in Madrid is a modern temple of late-night churro eating. So-called Spanish fritters appeared in early American cookbooks from colonial times, especially in Virginia, as one of the earliest donut recipes, alongside a recipe called Dough Nuts — a Yankee Cake.

Donut shops exist in Curaçao and the Philippines and Nigeria. And now American-style donuts have made it to China. They have become the People's Cake, an echo of the Chinese *pi* — the ring symbol that means eternity and luck as well as economic prosperity. My father went to install the first American donut machine in the first American model bakery in Beijing. With the U.S. Secretary of Agriculture, he was greeted with donuts made by Chinese workers from the new machine line. My father persuaded the

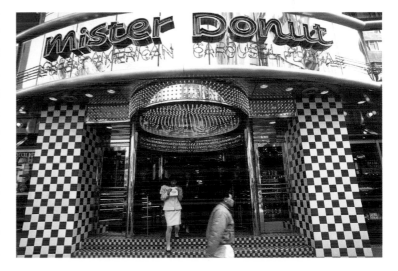

AROUND THE WORLD WITH DOUGHNUTS

Donuts are everywhere in the world from the United States to Saudi Arabia to Curaçao to China and Japan, where they are hugely popular.

Chinese by saying you can't have an American bakery without donuts. They agreed.

The winner in the global donut-eating game might be Japan, where there was no donut precedent, but where this American food became so popular that *Boston Globe* columnist Peter Behr said, "The donut . . . has established a junk food beachhead in Tokyo." The Donut King there had a real link to roy-

ALAIN DUCASSE, FRENCH DONUT MASTER

Alain Ducasse first wowed France with his three-star cuisine, complete with all-truffle menu. Then the three stars multiplied and became a collection, in Monte Carlo and Paris, and then in St.-Tropez and New York, from haute cuisine restaurants to bistros serving peanut butter and jelly and macaroni and cheese. Then there is his new gourmet shop in Paris, be, meaning *boulangerie/épicerie,* or bakery/grocery shop, where you can get ingredients to try at home, or dishes to take out and savor, and even donuts.

Here's what the chef has to say about it: "I like the doughnut because of its mellow [mellowness] and the easy way to accommodate it to all kind of garnishes (jam, cream, marmalade). For me, it is the perfect Anglo-Saxon 'gourmandise,' so I have decided to propose it in be, where it has a great success. In fact, I can easily eat around twenty, above all with jam that sticks to the face."

alty: The father of the Crown Princess was one of the moguls of the Japanese-American donut business. Japan also established a National Donut Month. The award winner of the Dunkin' Donuts world chain one year was a little lady in a kimono who did a million dollars' worth of business for the Yokohama Dunkin' Donuts shop.

The Mister Donut chain is also at the pinnacle of the donut empire in Japan. Mister Donut of Japan started when Seiichi Suzuki, formerly in dust control — mops and polish— came to the United States to learn franchising and met Harry Winokur of Mister Donut. Back in Tokyo, they met on the Ginza for lunch. The Americans ate rice, the Japanese ate bread, and Suzuki opened Mister Donut in Japan.

To test the viability of the shop, Mister Donut built a model shop in a warehouse. But the counters were too high, the chairs too large, the coffee cups too big, the donuts too heavy, the flavor too nutmeg. So, like Goldilocks, the owners tried until they got it right, which meant classier donuts than we sell in America, a more "glamorous" food, more expensive even, not the lowest common denominator. It also meant an emphasis on the Americanness of the donut — avoidance, for example, of anything Japanese, like bean paste filling. Even the signs were to be in English, not Japanese. Since the donut was an alien product, it needed a place not filled by

Ducasse Donuts with Red Fruit Compote

Here is a recipe for donuts as conceived by Alain Ducasse, the man many would call the world's greatest chef. *Makes 6 servings*

DONUTS

- 1 pound bread flour
- ⅓ cup superfine sugar, plus extra for coating
- 1 tablespoon instant yeast
- ¾ cup whole milk
- 10 tablespoons butter, softened
- Salt
- 4 eggs
- Vegetable oil for frying

1. Combine all the ingredients in the bowl of an electric mixer with a dough hook until the dough leaves the sides of the bowl cleanly. Let rise for 2 hours at room temperature.

2. On a floured surface, roll out the dough to 1¼ inches thick and cut out 4-inch disks. Make a 1¼-inch hole in the center of each one.

3. Transfer to one or more lightly floured baking sheets, well spaced out, and leave to rise at room temperature for 30 minutes.

4. Half-fill a deep fryer or tall, heavy saucepan with oil and heat to 355°F (180°C) and fry the donuts until golden brown. Transfer to paper towels to drain and then roll in super-fine sugar while still warm. Serve with the Red Fruit Compote.

RED FRUIT COMPOTE

- 1 gelatin leaf
- 1¼ pounds small strawberries
- 1 cup superfine sugar
- ¼ pound bilberries
- ¼ pound red currants
- ⅛ pound mulberries

1. Make the compote while dough is rising.

2. Soak gelatin in cold water to soften; drain.

3. Put the strawberries and 1 tablespoon of the sugar in the top of a double boiler over hot water and cover with plastic wrap to retain all their scent and flavor.

4. When the strawberries have released all their juice, push them through a conical sieve. Pour the juice back into the double boiler; add the gelatin and leave to dissolve.

5. Mix in the other fruits and the remaining sugar, and then cook over a medium heat for 3 to 5 minutes. Chill until required, stirring occasionally.

something Japanese, like tea and rice for breakfast. So it became a snack food, sold near trains and in supermarkets, and a Western product, along with other American cultural invaders like ketchup, jeans, and guitars.

THE ALL-AMERICAN DONUT,

From Fossil to Fasnacht to Today's Fast Food

The donut was there, which is something you cannot say for other American foods. The hot dog was not there for the Pilgrims as they descended from the ship. The colonists even had to do without bagels, whose hole was not punched out by Native American or whaler. Did the indigenous dwellers have apple pie, hamburgers?

As the settlers entered the New World, the Native Americans already had donuts. The Shawnees had the Shawneecake (which became johnnycake), a fried-dough cake of cornmeal somewhere between a pancake and a donut, often sweetened with sap. There are still recipes for Native American–style cornmeal donuts.

Proof of the existence of the Native American fried cake, even one with a hole, was dug up by Professor E. B. Reynard, of the University of Colorado Museum of Natural History. In a cave in Oklahoma full of the relics of a prehistoric tribe older than the Pueblo, he found a petrified donut with a hole in the middle, proving the donut a native. There is the tale of the Native American man who wanted to trade three of his women for the wife of a pioneer because he loved her donuts. The pioneer lady panicked, which led to a council of war. The settlement? A peace offering of a bushel of donuts to the Native American man. And another story tells that Aunt Sally and her mother had been boiling donuts in lard in upstate New York, where Native Americans still roamed on hunting trips. The women set the donuts on the stoop to cool, and when they went to get them they were gone. No one knew what had happened until a few days later, when a deer appeared where the donuts had been, as payment. Something about this country already loved a donut.

The donut began to make a name for itself in America. A few 18th-century recipes use the word *doughnut,* but it was in 19th-century America that the donut "came out." It appeared in major publications such as the *Miner's Journal* and the *Pittsburgh Workman.* In 1805 the *Pocumtuc Housewife* said that "gingerbread, seedcakes and doughnuts will suffice for daily needs." In 1835, *Harvardiana* refers to the "Yankee notion yclept doughnuts." And *Boston Monthly Magazine* said in 1826 that the "detestable" donut "sometimes resembles one of your inflexible little soup dumplings; at others it appears to be a kind of mongrel pancake."

Doughnuts

This recipe is from Susannah Carter, *The Frugal Housewife*, 1803.

To 1 pound flour, add ¼ pound butter, ¼ pound sugar, and 2 spoonfuls yeast; mix them all together in warm milk or water to the thickness of bread, let it raise, and make them in what form you please. Boil your fat (consisting of hog's lard) and put them in.

In the 1920s, *Good Housekeeping* refers to "the epitome of domestic bliss and family welfare, frying doughnuts."

In a book called *Food on the Frontier*, the two most popular frontier foods, agreed upon by all settlers on the American frontier, were coleslaw and donuts. Most of the groups of colonists brought some version of donuts to America, and no one knows who "done it" first. Washington Irving said it was the Dutch.

The well-known official "first" reference to

WHAT THEY SAID ABOUT DONUTS

1847, DRAKE'S PIONEER LIFE IN KENTUCKY: *"Other dainties awaited us as the result of killing hogs. They were 'doughnuts' and 'wonders,' the latter being known to you under the name of crullers."*

1847, THOREAU: *"The skylight . . . [was] the size of an oblong doughnut, and about as opaque."*

1859, MRS. CORNELIUS OF BOSTON IN YOUNG HOUSEKEEPER'S FRIEND: *"A person who fries cakes must attend to nothing else; the cakes, the fat and the fire will occupy every minute."*

1871, KNICKERBOCKER LIFE: *"The dames of Knickerbocker proclivities . . . had added the indigestible doughnut and cruller to the dyspepsia-provoking list."*

1889, ELLIOT'S NEW ENGLAND HISTORY: *". . . many a sweet thing was whispered behind a doughnut."*

donuts by their name, though the word existed before his stamp of authenticity appeared, is from Irving's tongue-in-cheek history of the early days of New York, *The History of New York from the Beginning of the World to the End of the Dutch Dynasty*, written in 1809 by the fictitious Diedrich Knickerbocker, Irving's eccentric creation. This was about early Dutch colonial days, the "honest" days in which "every woman staid at home, read the Bible, and wore pockets" for her scissors and pincushion. The reference marking the ceremonial debut of the donut into print is as follows:

> Sometimes the table was graced with immense apple pies or saucers full of preserved peaches and pears, but it was always sure to boast an enormous dish of balls of sweetened dough fried in hog's fat and called doughnuts, or olykoeks — a delicious kind of cake, at present scarce known in this city excepting in genuine Dutch families.

Again, in *The Legend of Sleepy Hollow*, he describes what was on the Dutch tea table: "There was the doughty doughnut, the tender 'olykoek' and the crisp and crumbling cruller." *Doughty* means "virtuous or manly." So that's what Irving thought of donuts.

The Dutch are also reputed to have had the first donut shop in the New World. There are late 18th-century recipes handwritten into copybooks by the Albany Dutch family the Van Rensselaers for cakes called "Oly-cooks" or "Very Common Snook-Kill Dough-nuts," proving that the word *doughnut* existed before Irving picked it up and made it official.

Some say that the Celtic tradition of giving fried cakes to widows and orphans on All Saints' Day traveled to America with the Pilgrims, who made fried cakes part of Halloween, when American ghosts and goblins scamper in the maple woods of New England in imitation of their ancestors, the wisps and spirits of Celtic glens. Later, October became National Donut Month, an incentive to witches on brooms to take a donut on their flight. But there is speculation among those who think the Pilgrims in New England brought donuts to America that even those donuts are really Dutch inspired. Since the Pilgrims were in Holland before they came to America, they are thought to have learned the art of donut making there before docking at Plymouth Rock.

The contender for the introduction of donuts to America is the Pennsylvania Dutch group, who were really Germans. In many of the early Pennsylvania newspapers, there are reports of holiday donuts, Christmas donuts carried to school, rabbit-shaped Easter donuts in lunch boxes, and especially Shrove Tuesday donuts. One comment about these donuts was that they were "not only a caution to the old folks, but must have been a great discomfort to

DONUTS FROM OUR PAST

Olykoek

This recipe is from the *Herald Tribune Cookbook*. The book says it is an early American favorite; the epicures of New Amsterdam soaked the olykoeks in Santa Cruz rum and served them with whipped cream.

Use a recipe for sweet rolls; cut off small pieces of dough and enclose brandied raisins or raisins and citron in center of each while shaping into small balls. Let stand until doubled. Fry in hot, deep fat (360°–370°F) for about 3 minutes, drain and roll in powdered sugar while warm.

Triangle Donuts

Pennsylvania Dutch Donuts

This recipe is from the *Gourmet Cookbook*. *Makes about 20 donuts*

3 large eggs
¼ cup granulated sugar
¼ cup cream
Generous grating of fresh nutmeg, or
    powdered cardamom seeds
Pinch of salt
About 3 cups cake flour
Deep fat or oil for deep frying
Confectioners' sugar

1. Beat eggs until foamy, add granulated sugar, and beat until well mixed. Add cream, nutmeg or cardamom, and salt to taste. Blend and sift in enough cake flour to make a soft dough.

2. Heat 3 to 4 inches of oil to 375°F in a tall, heavy saucepan.

3. Roll out dough until very thin on a floured board and cut it into narrow triangles about 5 inches long. In center of each make a cut about 1½ inches long and pull point of triangle through it.

4. Fry these twisted shapes in hot oil until they are lightly browned. Drain on paper towels and sprinkle with confectioners' sugar. Serve hot or cold.

the stomachs of the young ones." Shrove Tuesday Pennsylvania Dutch donuts became popular among Americans all over, some of the first to gain renown in the New World. Some even think they were the ancestor of the modern-day American donut. The Pennsylvania Dutch started the custom in this country of eating donuts, or fasnachts, as they called them, on the day before Lent. Shrove Tuesday became Fasnacht Day and later Donut Day among the Pennsylvania Dutch. People have said that the custom originated in the European pre-Christian spring rituals along the Rhine River in Germany, where the Pennsylvania Dutch came from and where donuts are still eaten.

In Pennsylvania Dutch Fasnacht Day celebrations, eating donuts ensures that you will live until the following Fasnacht Day. If you put the fasnacht fat on your hoe, it is magic, leading to a good harvest. The last person out of bed on Fasnacht Day is called a "lazy fasnacht" and gets only one donut.

The Shrove Tuesday custom of donut eating was also associated with the New Orleans beignet and with another fried cake, the rice donut, called the *cala*, also a pre-Lenten ritual, for the purpose of using up fat that was forbidden during Lent. The New Orleans French call Shrove Tuesday Mardi Gras, or Fat Tuesday. In Civil War days, black or Creole women hawked these donuts on the streets of New Orleans, chanting "Calas, tout chaud."

Some would say that the question of how donuts got to America does not end with the answer to who introduced them. Credit must surely also be given to those clever Salvation Army ladies in World War I who thought up the idea of frying donuts for the soldiers, who loved them so much that they asked for them when they got home. This led to the invention of the machine, which spread them across the plains and forests and main streets and back roads and into the public domain.

HOW THE DONUT GOT ITS HOLE

"None seemed to know why," says an article about the donut in the *Literary Digest* of 1916, "a portion of the atmosphere of just this shape and size should be surrounded by a circle of dough of just such satisfying thickness."

One story of how the donut got its hole came from an ancient pagan cult of the worship of Mercury, a wise leader-god who advised on love, life, language, money, and the future, in Greek times and after. One of the symbols of Mercury worship was a staff with two serpents twisted around it. This shape simplified became a ring with a hole in the middle, and the two shapes, ring and twist, were used for money and to symbolize Mercury. At feasts in Mercury's honor, cakes in these shapes were popular. Holidaymakers and seafarers carried them all over Europe.

Whether this story is true or not, the hole did not become an important feature of the donut until it got to America. Before that, donuts with holes were a minority group, but in this country they broke out of their under-privileged status and became a majority. The hole gave them a new look, so they gained visibility and a new American personality.

Upon its discovery, the American hole got a very enthusiastic reception from the press. The *Literary Digest* said, "We have built our civilization with Archimedes' lever, Newton's law of gravitation, Franklin's electricity; yet what would it be without Gregory's doughnut?"

One story tells of a Nauset brave who shot an arrow through the window of a log cabin in the early days of New England, into the kitchen where a Pilgrim wife was frying her cake in bear fat. The arrow slid into the cake and out the other side, belting out a hole in the middle. And so, says the story, the hole in the donut came of the interface of Native American and Pilgrim.

In another story a sea captain, Hanson Crockett Gregory, invented the hole in 1847 by sticking his cake onto the spoke of a ship's wheel in a storm. The frenzy of the storm caught him off guard, so he

CENTER HOLE.

Donuts can also be colorful, with or without sprinkles in rainbow colors.

Spiced Potato Donut

Here's a variation on the "spudnut," the old-fashioned American potato-based donut, a historic favorite on the American frontier, especially with the womenfolk who baked them for the "thrash gang," farmworkers in the wheat fields of the American prairies. From *Gourmet,* January 1990. *Makes about 20 donuts*

3½ cups all-purpose flour

4 teaspoons double-acting baking powder

1 teaspoon salt

2 teaspoons ground cinnamon

1 teaspoon freshly grated nutmeg

2 large eggs

3 tablespoons unsalted butter, melted

¾ cup sugar

1½ cups mashed cooked russet (baking) potatoes (about 1 pound)

½ cup milk

2 teaspoons freshly grated orange zest, if desired

1 teaspoon vanilla
Vegetable oil for frying

½ cup sugar

½ teaspoon ground cinnamon, or to taste

1. Into a bowl sift the flour, the baking powder, the salt, the cinnamon, and the nutmeg.

2. In a small bowl whisk together the eggs, the butter, the sugar, the potatoes, the milk, the zest, and the vanilla until the mixture is combined well; add the potato mixture to the flour mixture and stir the dough until it is just combined.

3. Chill the dough, covered, for 1 hour, or until it is cold and can be handled easily. Roll out half the dough ½ inch thick on a well-floured surface and with a 3- to 3½-inch doughnut cutter cut out doughnuts, reserving the center pieces.

4. Heat 2 inches of oil in a heavy pot to 375°F. Fry the doughnuts, and the reserved doughnut centers, in batches until they are golden, transferring them as they are fried to paper towels to drain.

5. In a shallow bowl stir together the sugar and the cinnamon.

6. While the doughnuts are still warm, roll them, one at a time, in the sugar mixture, coating them well.

slammed the cake down by accident onto the wheel, creating the first donut hole. Pleased with his convenient creation, which could rest on a ship's wheel at a moment's notice, the captain ordered more cakes with holes from the ship's cook. Some have variations for this tale: Cap'n Gregory had lost six men overboard after they had eaten soggy fried cakes, which made them so heavy they sank to the bottom; or he was inspired by the life preserver hanging on his boat and wanted his fried cakes to look like edible life preservers. Or when Cap'n Gregory saw his mother frying cakes in her kitchen, they came out with uncooked centers, so he poked them out with a fork or his finger to leave a hole.

An interview between reporter Carl Wilmore and Gregory appeared in the *Boston Post* at the turn of the century. It said that in 1847 Gregory was aboard a schooner called the *Isaac Achorn,* in the lime trade, eating tough, greasy fried cakes and "twisters." He had been pondering the problem of digesting the "greasy sinkers" when he asked himself, "Why wouldn't a space inside solve the difficulty?" Suddenly, "I took the cover off the ship's tin pepper box, and — I cut into the middle of that doughnut the first hole ever seen by mortal eyes." Then he proceeded to say that actually he had "discovered" the existence of the hole and then had simply "invented the proper method of enclosing such a hole in an adequate doughnut." Then,

bashful, he added, "Of course, a hole ain't so much, but it's the best part of the doughnut — you'd think so if you had ever tasted the doughnuts we used to eat." The reporter asked if Gregory was pleased. Gregory's reply: "Was Columbus pleased?"

A plaque in his hometown "proves" Cap'n Gregory the inventor of the hole. It says:

The Inventor of the Hole in the Doughnut
Captain Hanson Crockett Gregory
Born, Clam Cove, Maine, 1832
Died, Quincy, Massachusetts, 1921

Captain Gregory is said to have invented the hole in the donut aboard a ship in a storm.

There are those who say the real hole was invented by the inventor of the donut cutter, a certain John Blondel. In 1872 he fashioned a metal tube that forced out a ring of dough. There are those who say that the Native American was the true inventor and that innumerable floats in parades showing Native American warriors shooting arrows through donuts proved it.

But for the "hole" truth, you must refer to the annals of the Great Doughnut Debate, held in 1941 in New York at the Hotel Astor, right before the attack on Pearl Harbor. Clifton Fadiman and Elsa Maxwell were among the judges. The subject? "Who Put the Hole in the Doughnut?" The debaters? Fred E. Crockett of Camden, Maine, who defended Captain Gregory, his relative. There is disagreement about who defended the Native American. Some say it was a tribal chief with a Harvard Ph.D. Others say it was Cape Cod "historian" Louis P. De Gouy, who is said to have written up the shooting of the fried cake by the Native American. Most, including *Smithsonian* magazine, say it was Henry Ellis, Cape Cod attorney, defending his local Nauset brave. The evidence? Ellis had only arguments. Crockett, however, produced documents and affidavits. The winner? Captain Gregory, hands down. Later, the admission of Henry Ellis: "It was all a gag. I've told that story so many times I almost believe it myself."

THE "HOLE" TRUTH ABOUT DONUTS

I set out on a sleuthing job to get the "real" story of the hole. The relative who had defended Cap'n Gregory at the debate, I heard, was still alive in the wilds of New England. He had produced documents at the debate, so I thought he might know the "hole" truth and clear up the mystery forever. He would be the last survivor of this illustrious donut personage, perhaps the most famous name in donuts. So I went to the library and got out the phone book for the county in Maine where I had heard Cap'n Gregory came from. I looked up all the people who

A plaque in Captain Gregory's hometown "proves" that he invented the hole in the donut.

had any of his three names, Hanson, Crockett, Gregory. I called the librarian at the Camden Public Library, and the Chamber of Commerce there. I spoke to *Down East* magazine and to the *Camden Herald*. I spoke to Ye Olde New England Kitchen Bakery. I found the brother, the sister, the cousin, and the aunt of Fred Crockett, the famous defender of the inventor of the hole. They told me where Fred was. His sister was nice but didn't know much about donuts and holes. His brother was very helpful. He said he thought Fred should talk to me and that I should tell him that. I found out from them that Fred's father was the second cousin of Cap'n Gregory, and that's how Fred got into the debate. I found out that a plan to erect a statue of Gregory on top of a mountain in Maine never went through but that the Rockport Lutheran Church has a plaque commemorating him. I found out that Cap'n Gregory was the youngest sea captain off the Maine coast and that he was born in Clam Cove, Maine, and died in Quincy, Massachusetts. I found him pictured on a map of Maine in the *World Book Encyclopedia* with donuts and a life preserver around his foot. Underneath was "Invention of the Donut Hole in 1847 by Captain Hanson Gregory is still commemorated at Camden." Gregory also had a second career in bravery at sea, saving Spanish sailors and getting a medal from the Spanish queen. Was it those holey donuts?

The best documentation for Gregory as a "real" person comes from *Down East* magazine, May 1967. One relative, a grandniece, remembers that Gregory poked out the leaden centers of his mother's fried cakes. Another remembers that he introduced the donut with hole on his whaling voyages all

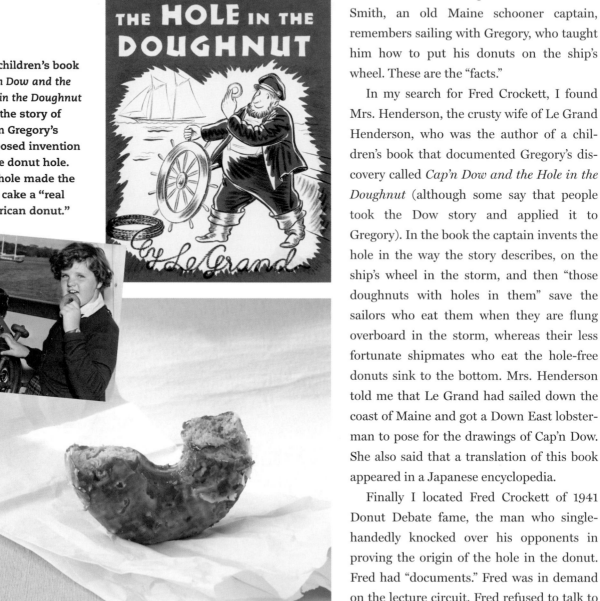

The children's book *Cap'n Dow and the Hole in the Doughnut* tells the story of Cap'n Gregory's supposed invention of the donut hole. The hole made the fried cake a "real American donut."

over the world, on ships with names like *Hard Scrabble* and *Cephus Starret*. Alonzo Smith, an old Maine schooner captain, remembers sailing with Gregory, who taught him how to put his donuts on the ship's wheel. These are the "facts."

In my search for Fred Crockett, I found Mrs. Henderson, the crusty wife of Le Grand Henderson, who was the author of a children's book that documented Gregory's discovery called *Cap'n Dow and the Hole in the Doughnut* (although some say that people took the Dow story and applied it to Gregory). In the book the captain invents the hole in the way the story describes, on the ship's wheel in the storm, and then "those doughnuts with holes in them" save the sailors who eat them when they are flung overboard in the storm, whereas their less fortunate shipmates who eat the hole-free donuts sink to the bottom. Mrs. Henderson told me that Le Grand had sailed down the coast of Maine and got a Down East lobsterman to pose for the drawings of Cap'n Dow. She also said that a translation of this book appeared in a Japanese encyclopedia.

Finally I located Fred Crockett of 1941 Donut Debate fame, the man who singlehandedly knocked over his opponents in proving the origin of the hole in the donut. Fred had "documents." Fred was in demand on the lecture circuit. Fred refused to talk to me. Finally, after I pestered him, he agreed to come to the phone but would not grant an interview, because, he said, people have taken advantage of him. He said he had a scrapbook on his ancestor the sea captain, who made it big in donut holes, and on his own rise to glory as defender of the donut faith, but that he would not show it to me. He agreed to send me some "top secret" material, which turned out to be an article I already had about a donut festival in Maine with Senator Muskie. I told him his brother's advice that he should talk to me. I implored him with my best wiles about invaluable scholarly resources and future TV fame, but he was the one person in all my searches who would not see me. The single fact he divulged was that he had made up a Donut Navy, including Mae West, Gloria Vanderbilt, and President Eisenhower, but in all my research I found no other mention of this, so I don't know if it existed outside of Fred's head. One of Fred's relatives said, "There's a lot to be cleared up before we straighten this out."

So there it is, a subject with no entries in the card catalog, and the one living connection to historical "proof" who would not talk to me. Research so "original" that not only do you have to make up how to collect facts and sort them, but you have to try to find out if there are facts at all. That's how I discovered that doing research on donuts is different from doing research on, say, Elizabethan dramas or the survival of the Komodo dragon.

New Orleans Calas

The recipe for these Creole donuts comes from the *Gourmet Cookbook*. *Makes 12–15 donuts*

- ½ cup rice
- 1 package or cake of yeast
- 3 eggs, well beaten
  About 3 tablespoons flour
- ½ cup sugar
- ½ teaspoon salt
  Pinch of nutmeg
  Vegetable oil for deep frying

1. Cook rice in 3 cups boiling water until very soft; drain and cool.

2. Soften yeast in 2 tablespoons warm water. Combine rice with yeast and let sponge stand overnight in a warm place.

3. Add eggs to rice. Add 3 tablespoons of the flour, the sugar, salt, and nutmeg to taste and beat well. Add more flour, if necessary, to make a thick batter.

4. Heat oil in a heavy pan to 370°F. Drop dough by tablespoons into the hot oil and fry until the doughnuts are golden brown. Drain, sprinkle with sugar, and serve hot.

Four

WHAT CAN A DONUT BE?

Some people might think donuts are a mass of molecules turned into dough and shoved into cake shape, round with a hole, good to eat. But anyone who thinks a minute longer will know that nothing in life is that easy. There's more to the donut than meets the eye, even more than you can look at through the hole. Although Everyman likes donuts as food, they have become more than they seem to be and more than their taste. We have seen that they were, from early times, a ritual food associated with holidays and with rites of life and death, with thanksgiving and luck. From their biblical status as thanksgiving objects to their appearance as symbols of rebirth in German spring celebrations to their guarantee of another year of life on Shrove Tuesday in Pennsylvania, donuts have meanings beyond their edible matter, and they exercise special influence over events.

In America, because of their vast popularity, they have become a part of folklore. Rising above dessert or snack, they have come to represent this land.

Donuts as circles represent a basic visual element of life, nature, and the universe, as well as one of the shapes people have used as symbols from the beginning. The circle is a fact of life and a suggestion of ultimate concerns. Everywhere the eye falls there are circles, in the sky, on the ground, in bodies heavenly and human, in nature and in culture. Since caveman times people have drawn them, thought of them, used them to represent things and ideas. As an embodiment of the circle, the donut also has the power to suggest other things. It has come to symbolize the universe and the universal themes of perfection and harmony, the cycle of life, death, and rebirth.

The donut has captured people's minds as well as their hearts and tongues. From sugary circle held in the hand, the donut migrates to the brain to form images that repeat and repeat everywhere. When people eat donuts, the unconscious cosmic donut, the circle, is there, echoing the Milky Way, the lover's symbol, the magician's charm, as well as more

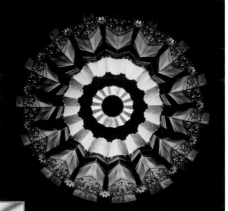

philosophical notions of time and space, being and nonbeing. A Zen monk wrote a meditation on the donut called "Mystical and Metaphysical Qualities of an Average but Unknown Donut: Conclusions Resulting from Meditation and Contemplation." A mathematician uses donuts in his discussion of concepts of change and permanence. The donut image has been used to describe a mechanical airplane part

THE UNIVERSAL DONUT

Man-made donuts are everywhere. The donut-shaped flying saucer, below, did not get far from the ground. Looking into a kaleidoscope, we see — a donut!

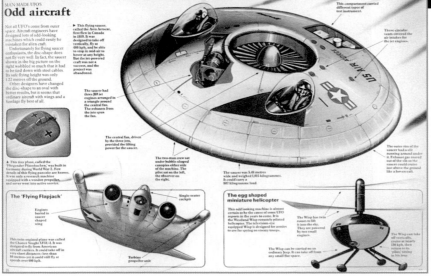

MAN-MADE UFO'S
Odd aircraft

Not all UFO's come from outer space. Aircraft engineers have designed lots of odd-looking machines which could easily be mistaken for alien craft. Unfortunately for flying saucer enthusiasts, the disc-shape does not fly very well. In fact, the saucer shown in the big picture on the right wobbled so much that it had to be tied down with steel cables. Its safe flying height was only 1.22 metres off the ground. Other designers have changed the disc-shape to an oval with better results, but it seems that ordinary aircraft with wings and a fuselage fly best of all.

▶ This flying saucer, called the Avro Avrocar, first flew in Canada in 1959. It was designed to take off vertically, fly at 480 kph, and be able to stop in mid-air to hover at any height. But the jet-powered craft was not a success, and the project was abandoned.

This compartment carried different types of test instrument.

These circular vents covered the air intakes for the jet engines.

The saucer had three jet engines arranged in a triangle around the central fan. The exhausts from the jets spun the fan.

The central fan, driven by the three jets, provided the lifting power for the saucer.

The two-man crew sat under bubble-shaped canopies either side of the machine. The pilot sat on the left, the observer on the right.

The saucer was 5.48 metres wide and weighed 1,815 kilogrammes. It could carry a 907 kilogramme load.

The outer rim of the saucer had a slit running around under it. Exhaust gas roared out of the slit so the saucer could cruise just above the ground like a hovercraft.

▲ This tiny plane, called the 'Flugunder Pfannkuchen,' was built in Germany during World War 2. Few details of this flying pancake are known. It was only a research machine equipped with a wooden propeller and never went into active service.

The 'Flying Flapjack'

Engines buried in saucer shaped wing

Single-seater cockpit

This twin-engined plane was called the Chance Vought XF5U-1. It was designed to fly from American aircraft carriers. It could take off in very short distances—less than 50 metres—yet it could still fly at speeds over 800 kph.

Turbine propeller unit

The egg shaped miniature helicopter

This odd looking machine is almost certain to be the cause of some UFO reports in the years to come. It is the Westland Wisp remotely piloted helicopter. The television-eye equipped Wisp is designed for armies to use for spying on enemy troops.

The Wisp has twin rotors to lift it into the sky. They are powered by two small engines.

The Wisp can be carried in an ordinary Jeep. It can take off from any small flat space.

The Wisp can take off vertically, cruise at nearly 130 kph, then return to its 'pilot,' sitting in his Jeep.

and a nuclear reactor. The donut has traveled in many "circles," from roadside stand to astronomical theory, from object to image to abstraction, an example of our ability to make symbols from the things we see.

Donuts are thus part of our conceptual culture. They are comestible, but they are also ritual and symbolic and metaphorical. They are part of pop culture and of religious and social life. One donut, the Chock Full O'Nuts Whole Wheat Donut, has even been likened to the Holy Grail. Donuts are images and conceptualizations, not just material artifacts or objects to eat. They serve to explain the world, and they are part of it.

Because of its conjunction of circularity and popularity and its particular appeal to the imagination, the donut has become a unique multifaceted symbol, in addition to its status as an American icon. It lends itself to speculation and to lore. As an instantly recognizable image, the universal donut is lifted from triviality into other realms of human experience. Space-time donuts, topological donuts, meditational donuts. What other food has such connections? To those who accuse donuts of being the ultimate trivia, it should be said that they can be ultimate, as well as trivia.

I remember when my father brought home his first Chinese "donut" from Hong Kong, long before American donuts went to China.

It was a ring of jade carved with a relief of swirling dragons and curlicue clouds. "What's that? A donut?" we asked. "Mmm. Something to rub. A paperweight, maybe." Actually, it was a Chinese *pi,* a symbol of eternal life and other ultimate concerns. The pi is the oldest known donut shape. The Chinese were the first to use it in human culture.

A Chinese jade *pi* is one of the oldest donut shapes in human culture, a symbol of eternal life.

DONUTS IN THE MEDIA

From Charles Kupchan on *PBS News,* April 29, 2003: "I think we're in a very fluid period where both the United States and various European countries are trying to take stock, figure out how much damage has been done, figure out where the Atlantic alliance can be repaired. . . . That leaves what is called the doughnut alliance, the smaller countries in the rim land of Europe, to make some critical choices."

From *Nova,* PBS: "Kuiper Belt — a doughnut-shaped region of comets in orbit beyond Neptune, assumed to be the oldest surviving remnant of the original solar nebula and the source of short-period comets."

From Kathleen Cleaver on PBS: "So many cities have this, what you call 'doughnut shape.' In the middle is a little black hole. And all on the outside, it's all the wealth and the tax money and the resources, where white people live."

One of the world's most ancient symbols is the *uroboros*, the snake in a circle biting its tail, which was known in places as widely scattered as the ancient civilizations of Babylon, Egypt, Mexico, Phoenicia, India, and Rome. A philosopher explains this particular image: "Living the cycle of its own life, it is the circular snake, the primal dragon of the beginning that bites its own tail, the self-begetting uroboros . . . It is man and woman . . . active and passive." Annie Dillard, prophet of nature, talks of this snake image when she finds a snakeskin tied into a continuous loop, and then the ubiquitous donut enters the discussion. "I couldn't untie it any more than I could untie a doughnut . . . These snakes are magic . . . Time is the continuous loop, the snakeskin with scales endlessly overlapping . . . The power we seek too seems to be a continuous loop." Another donut, continuous in time and space.

Philosophers fastened on the circle as "one symbol of original perfection . . . no before and no after." In his book *The Origins and History of Consciousness*, Erich Neumann writes, "So long as man shall exist, perfection will continue to appear as the circle, the sphere, and the round." It is no wonder that the circle, then, has come to signify harmony in the cosmos, the harmony of the spheres, and harmony in human life, as well as eternity and the cycle of life. Donuts are reminders of these aspects of life. Ernst Gombrich, the art historian, has pointed to the use of ordered images, the circle in particular, to reflect inner states. He describes a dream of a circle at a time of chaos that led to peace and to a decision. Carl Jung found that a recurrent dream image is the mandala, a circular arrangement of figures, from the Sanskrit word for magic circle. The mandala is one example of the circles that have suggested harmony and peace from the oldest religions, from primitive sun wheel to Indian bodhisattvas (Buddhas-to-be, often represented in a circle), from meditational aid in yoga to Christ in a circle of figures and symbols. In less spiritual realms, the kaleidoscope gains its appeal from ordering fragmented images into a circle. And Mickey Mouse is nothing but "a conjunction of happy circles," Disney's favorite shape because they are "friendly, non-threatening."

The circle as symbol is based on the actual circles that are fundamental to the heavens and nature. If Einstein is right about the curvature of space, maybe space is a big donut with lots of munchkins floating in it. Ellipses govern the movements of heavenly bodies. Saturn has rings. We see the circle of the sun around us, though it is an illusion. There are man-made circles all over our planet — longitude and latitude, equator and horizon — measuring our whereabouts, ringing our view. The earth has nautical circles and polar circles and donut-shaped magnetic fields.

The *uroboros*, a snake biting its tail (this page), suggests the cycle of life. The donut-shaped *tokamak* (opposite) is a fusion device for producing energy.

DEUTERIUM NUCLEUS   TRITIUM NUCLEUS   HELIUM-4 NUCLEUS   NEUTRON

In a fusion reaction, a nucleus of hot deuterium gas may combine with one of tritium to produce helium — releasing one extremely energetic neutron

PATH OF SPEEDING PARTICLES

HOROZONTAL MAGNETIC FIELD

VERTICAL MAGNETIC FIELD

Diagram of a tokamak, an advanced fusion device: Nuclei — confined in a doughnut-shaped chamber by two magnetic fields (one horizontal, one vertical) that are generated by electric current — speed around and collide.

Moon Rocks (chocolate donut muffins)

Lora Brody, American superchef, cookbook author, and one-woman food brand, has written dozens of books about food, including *Growing Up on the Chocolate Diet* and *The Cape Cod Table*. This is her donut recipe, with its surprising name. "I named them because they look like my idea of what moon rocks look like," she says. *Makes 24 mini-muffins*

MOON ROCKS

Butter for coating the pan

6 ounces (1½ sticks) unsalted butter

4 ounces unsweetened chocolate, chopped

2½ cups all-purpose flour

¼ cup Dutch-processed cocoa

½ teaspoon salt

2 teaspoons baking soda

2 teaspoons baking powder

1 cup granulated sugar

2 extra large eggs

¾ cup sour cream

1. Preheat the oven to 350°F. Lavishly butter a 24-cup mini-muffin pan.

2. Melt the butter and chocolate together in either a microwave oven or double boiler. Stir until smooth, remove from heat, and allow to cool to room temperature.

3. Sift the flour, cocoa, salt, baking soda, and baking powder into a small bowl and set aside. Place the eggs and sugar in the bowl of an electric mixer and beat on high until thick and light yellow in color (about 5 minutes).

4. With the mixer on low speed, add the chocolate/butter mixture, and when it is incorporated, add the dry ingredients, mixing until they are nearly blended. Add the sour cream and mix quickly and thoroughly, scraping down the sides of the bowl with a rubber scraper. The mixture will be thick and slightly fizzy.

5. Immediately pile enough batter into each muffin hole to reach the top.

6. Bake the muffins for 15 to 17 minutes, or until the tops are shiny and cracked and the inside is dry when a cake tester or toothpick is inserted.

GLAZE

While the moon rocks are baking, prepare the glaze:

- 1⅓ cups confectioners' sugar, sifted
- 6 tablespoons melted unsalted butter
- 2 tablespoons hot water

Add all the ingredients to a small bowl and whisk until smooth.

TO COMPLETE

As soon as the moon rocks come out of the oven, turn each on its side to allow the bottom and sides to cool for 5 minutes. As soon as they are cool enough to handle and while they are still hot, dip the top of each muffin into the glaze, coating the top heavily enough so that when you invert the moon rock, some of the glaze runs down the sides. Set the moon rocks right-side up on a wire rack or sheet pan to cool.

Do dogs dunk?

One of Math's Major Problems Reported Solved

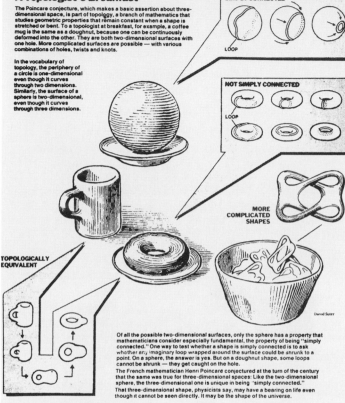

SCIENTIFIC STUDIES AND THE DONUT

The scientific study of topology has espoused the idea that the donut is one of the two basic shapes in the universe (the other is the sphere), and that, in fact, the universe itself is shaped like a donut, called a torus. A recent description by George Johnson in the *New York Times* is that the universe is "a kind of hyper-doughnut, or so it would appear to a four-dimensional being standing outside of creation and viewing it whole." Another article, titled "Universe as Doughnut," discusses the latest theories of the shape of the universe based on satellite data suggesting that the universe is finite and therefore might resemble a donut. One of the scientists quoted in the article, Dr. Glenn Starkman, says, "We're looking for circles in the sky." Donuts have also proved useful in describing not only the universe but also minute constituents of matter, like nuclei, that might also be shaped like rings, according to James Glanz.

Thus the torus, or donut, is thought by some scientists to be the shape of both the universe and its smallest particle. One mathematician says, "Whether we deal with the particle or the universe of particles, the topology is toroidal; their difference is in their time scale." This theorist also says that the torus, or donut, connects the individual to the universe: "The self, in a toroidal universe, can be both separate and connected with the rest of the universe. And the problem is the same for many selves which would constitute more holes; a hole for each but all connected."

In *Bridges to Infinity*, the mathematician Michael Guillen used the donut in his theory of "topological equivalence," part of a discussion of mathematical theories of change and permanence. One of these, catastrophe theory, is "elaborated in the language of topol-

TWO OBJECTS ARE SAID TO BE TOPOLOGICALLY EQUIVALENT *if they share certain essential attributes, regardless of their other dissimilarities. For instance, a doughnut and a coffee cup are topologically equivalent because each has a hole in it. The hole is an essential feature in the sense that if we imagine transfiguring a doughnut into a cup or vice versa, almost everything else about the object will have changed in the process except for the hole; it persists. Topological equivalence is always judged on the basis of such immutable (qualitative) attributes only, not mutable (quantitative) details such as the size of the doughnut or the specific shape of the cup. For this reason, it is possible, and even common, for two very different-looking objects to be topologically equivalent . . .*

In developing catastrophe theory, Thom set out to find an analogous way of qualitatively relating catastrophes, even ones that might be as outwardly dissimilar as cups and doughnuts. For this reason he sought an analogy to the hole, some essential attribute of catastrophes that might be used to mathematically describe and classify them.

— Michael Guillen, *Bridges to Infinity*

ogy, the qualitative mathematical study of shapes."

The physicist Len Fisher takes a different scientific look at the donut in a book called *How to Dunk a Doughnut: The Science of Everyday Life*, showing the science behind ordinary activities. Fisher says, "I started out with biscuit dunking, but doughnuts sounded more mellifluous."

Len Fisher sets out to explain the behavior of atoms and molecules:

Some of the first evidence about that behavior came from scientists who were trying to understand the forces that suck liquids into porous materials. One of the most common manifestations of this effect is when coffee is drawn into a dunked doughnut. . . . Doughnuts might have been designed for dunking. A doughnut, like bread, is held together by an elastic net of the protein gluten. The gluten might stretch, and eventually break, when the doughnut is dunked in hot coffee, but it doesn't swell or dissolve as the liquid is drawn into the network of holes and channels that the gluten supports. This means that the doughnut dunker can take his or her time, pausing only to let the excess liquid drain back into the cup before raising the doughnut to the waiting mouth. The only problem that the doughnut dunker faces is the selection of the doughnut.

After discussing the technicalities of dunking doughnuts versus cookies, Fisher says, "The science of dunking may seem trivial. . . . To myself and other scientists, though, asking 'why?' is one of the most serious things that we can do."

Nature abounds with donuts. It is the shape by which motion can exist in a medium, air in air, or water in water, the tornado and the whirlpool. A tornado is a donut of air. It is called a twister and so are donuts. The donut is one of the basic shapes in nature. A volcano with crater. A sea with an island for a hole. A lake ringed with mountains. The trilobite, a mollusk ancestor of the horseshoe crab, had donut-shaped eyes all over its shell. The necks of birds have rings on them. A pebble dropped in water makes a series of concentric ripples. Mushrooms can sometimes grow in circles in the woods. This has been called a fairy ring, and it's not an accident, scientists say. It abides by a natural law, the "halo effect of a field of force in nature, a circular surround [that] sets off the center." Flower petals around pollen or colored circles around the parts of animal bodies are part of this law. Nature forms circles and we find them. Donuts remind us of nature and its phenomena. They are part of discovering the world. How clever of humankind to invent an edible that echoes nature in its shape, kindling our imagination as well as filling the belly.

We repeat nature in culture. We grant approval by holding up a rounded forefinger meeting thumb, a donut of fingers. A target is a donut, and the bull's-eye is nothing other than the hole. We make the letter *o*, and between plus and minus we put another donut, zero. We make circus rings and angels' halos and rubber tires. A laurel wreath is a donut. The Olympic symbol is five donuts linked to represent the continents. In fact, one year a T-shirt was created for the Olympics with five linked donuts on it and the caption "Dough"-lympics underneath. We wear wedding rings and we worry about crime rings. One of the early names of donuts came from a medieval finger ring. Circles and rings came to have magical properties, associations with superstition and luck as well as worship. Rings blessed by kings could dispel pain, and rings with secret chambers filled with poison eliminated people. Conjurers used rings against the devil and evil spirits in charms. Soothsayers used them to prophesy. The ring-shaped donut also has its magic, ensuring a good harvest, rebirth, good luck, and another year of life.

An exhibit on Mayan culture displayed mystery objects that challenged the viewer to become an archaeologist and discover their use. One of the actual mysteries, whose use is truly unknown, was the ring-shaped stone people called the Donut Stone. Guesses of the viewing public ranged from a grinding stone

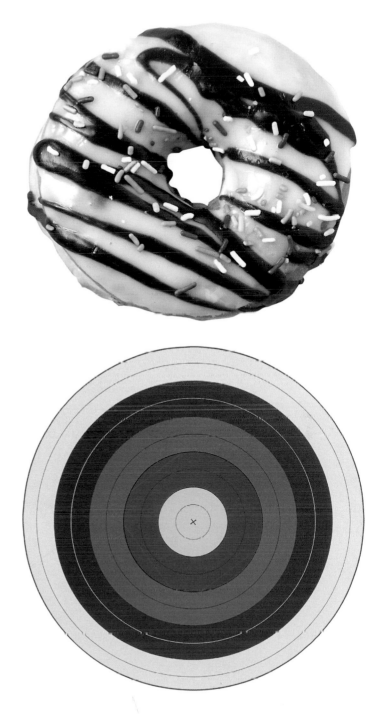

Mind of the Raven: *The Donut IQ Test*

Who knew donuts would also be a way birds could prove how smart they are? In an experiment with ravens, donuts acted as instruments of proof. Using its bill as storage tool or hanger, a raven utilized a donut's hole to facilitate long-range transport of the desired commodity to a safe haven, a more beneficial vantage point for maximizing the potential of the food find, the donut. David Quammen reviewed *Mind of the Raven*, by Bernard Heinrich, for the *New York Times*:

> *Norse legend tells that Odin, lord of the gods, was attended by two ravens, named Hugin (Thought) and Munin (Memory), who served him as reconnaissance agents, returning after each long, snoopy flight to perch on his shoulders and whisper into his ears. The story reflects a widespread belief, spanning cultures and centuries, that ravens possess uncanny intelligence. By actual measurement they are the brainiest of birds . . .*
>
> *It began with a hearsay report that an oil pipeline worker in Alaska had tossed two doughnuts to a pestering raven, curious to see whether that windfall would confuse the bird. Rather than gorging on a single doughnut, or taking one away to cache while leaving the other at risk, the raven had stuck its bill through the first doughnut's hole, grasped the second with its bill tip and flown away with both . . . Did the peekaboo doughnut grab constitute analytic problem-solving? Could it be replicated by any of the hand-reared ravens at his field camp in western Maine? . . . A raven named Fuzz did manage to carry two doughnuts at once, one serving as a basket for the other, though none of his birds hit upon the peekaboo grab. Heinrich says of the Maine ravens, "if they seemed a little more idiosyncratic or creative than the Alaskan raven, it was probably because the Alaskan pipeline workers eat bigger doughnuts than those from the Koffee Kup Bakery."*

to a weight to a coin to a petrified donut. Real archaeologists think it was used either as a door hinge, or as a part of a digging stick, or as a weight for a fishing net.

The donut is there when something else needs describing, anything from a storm to a stone to a mathematical idea. One of the most outlandish and up-to-date donut images was recently heard on *CBS Radio News*. Noting the unfortunate effects of speaking on cell phones in cars, Dave Ross put it this way: "A cell phone is a donut with a dial tone." Donuts are even used to call someone a name — "You donut, you!"

Spacetime Donuts, a science-fiction book by the mathematician Rudy Rucker, discusses theories of the universe by using the concept of donut-shaped spheres, a crazy mix of Einstein, science fiction, and philosophy.

Not space-time bagels or space-time apple pie. Bagels are not as well suited to represent the shape of the cosmos, abstracted from their gastronomy and ethnicity, from their performance in delis and at Sunday brunches. They are stuck in the suburbs. Apple pie has attained status beyond itself mainly by association with Mother, with the warm aroma of childhood and homey times, when the hearth smelled better than it does in these days of microwave ovens and DVDs. Donuts, on the other hand, partake of it all — hearth and home, brunch and rally, fast food, high tech, and heaven too.

MAN, WHAT ARE YOU TALKING ABOUT?

". . . basically the idea is that space-time plus scale looks like a doughnut."

"And that's supposed to be the universe or what?" Vernor continued enthusiastically. "It's like each one of those circles is a size level. The first level is human level, then you shrink on down to the atomic level, the little circle around the hole. Next you get up to the level of the big universe when you hit the equator — the circle around the outside of the doughnut."

The science-fiction book *Spacetime Donuts* describes donut-shaped spheres as the basis for a theory of the universe.

VIEW THROUGH THE DONUT HOLE

Kids love looking at things through a donut hole.

WHAT'S IN THE HOLE?

Considering the donut, someone will ask, "Which came first, the donut or the hole?"

Everyone assumes the donut was first, and then someone poked a hole in it. To make a hole in a solid you need a "stick," something to poke with. So people thought up "stick stories." Here the stick is an Indian's arrow shot into a cake. There the stick is the spoke of a ship's wheel someone rammed the cake onto. Or Captain Gregory's finger. Then, given the fact of cake-with-hole, people want to know more. Something about the hole causes speculation, fantasy, imagination, philosophy, even. Why is the hole empty? Or is it? Is it full of something? Air? What do you do with it? How do you eat a donut — around the hole? What if it didn't have a hole? Would a donut have become a donut without a hole? People always want to know how the hole happened. The hole fascinates.

Watch children as they eat a donut. At some point a finger goes through the hole, wiggles out the other side, emerges sticky and crumb laden, the universal urge to stick things in holes. An eye looks through the hole. "Look, Mom, a telescope!" I often think the donut is an answer to children's desires to poke their fingers into and through things. Not just children. There is a universal urge to make holes in things without them, to put sticks in things with them. People want to look through holes or fill them up. If there is a hole, curiosity leads us to look through. A hole encloses a secret. Sometimes people make holes to draw people to look at something they might walk right by if they could see it all before them, as when passersby look through the holes of a wall blocking construction from a busy street. Those holes are filled with the gazes of curious onlookers who would not even have turned their heads had there been no wall-with-hole to look through. Looking through a hole frames the picture, presents a view different from the panorama before our eyes. Everyone wants to see what is partly hidden. A hole is a way to see in. Hiding makes people want to know. This urge causes people to keep things secret that are hardly worth telling.

The hole is part of "The Joy of Donuts." Does the urge to look through come from our first look through the "original" hole as we entered the world? It's hard not to think of body parts when you look at donuts. Once you think of this, you see reminders of the anatomy everywhere around donuts. Without mentioning this, I asked my father why he thought people liked donuts. "Easy," he said. "Their shape." (He didn't say, "Their taste.") And then, "You know what I'm thinking of starting? A chain of shops where they sell three things together — donuts, hog dogs, and soft ice cream." Then I thought of the maple sugaring snack: donut, pickle, and snow with maple syrup eaten together at "sugaring off" time. Same motif. The stick and hole again.

Was Yeats thinking of donuts and holes in his poem "The Second Coming," which contains the line, "The center cannot hold"?

All you need is a donut, and the imagination soars into spirals and tangents, flights of fancy and carnivals and masked balls. Ask anyone what she thinks about donuts, and you will find things hidden inside donuts and inside the person too, a variety of reactions. Like an inkblot test — show the donut, find out what people see there.

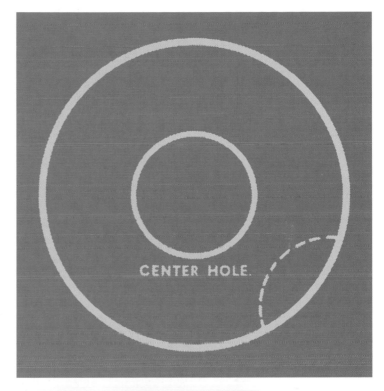

CENTER HOLE.

MYSTICAL DONUTS? "The circle is a whole but also a hole" (above) from a Zen meditation. A tourist touches a huge stone carved in a donut shape on the Yap Islands (left).

PRETTY IN PINK

Pink donuts are so . . . well, pink!! Fresh raspberries color some donut glazes at New York City's Doughnut Plant (above). Or you might want to add sprinkles (right).

DONUT MORPHS

What can a donut be? Almost anything, it seems. A Chinese jewel box, a gourmet dessert, a gallery window, the universe. Donuts morph, they are versatile; they are satisfying and sublime, infinitely variable, and soothingly and eternally universal.

Donuts are round, right? Not necessarily. Not in see-and-be-seen St.-Tropez, France, where you can lunch and swim beside Jack Nicholson, Naomi Campbell, Bruce Willis, and other luminaries. The boys on the beach with boxes strapped around their necks sell beignets — jelly- or chocolate-filled donuts — and they are . . . rectangles!

So, can we design a donut in whatever shape we please? Conceptualize a donut in a

different way? Donuts as, say, the crust on a dessert pizza? Or donuts on top of apple pie (to keep it in the American family)?

A donut is a donut, or not. When is a donut not a donut? Here are some wrong answers:

1. When it's a hole.
2. When it's square.
3. When it has jalapeño in it.
4. When it's not sweet.

Filled donuts are nothing new, but what about a flower-shaped donut with seafood stuffing? When he was restaurant reviewer for the *New York Times*, William Grimes described the following dish at the new Biltmore Room restaurant: "The Biltmore crab cake, cleverly disguised as a stuffed squash blossom, took me completely by surprise. The squash blossom, fried to a crisp, provided the necessary exterior crunch, a textural contrast to the creamy filling of crab meat in béchamel sauce. It is a seafood doughnut, really."

DONUT STYLE

Who knows, maybe the donut will be — jewelry. I saw a guy in New York with a jester outfit made of old fabric scraps, and a floppy hat. He was wearing a pendant, which was a CD, a kind of metal donut complete with hole. Why not a real donut? A French Web site has evidence that the idea of donuts-as-jewelry is not so far-fetched as you might think. This site sells hand-cut stone donuts, called Les Doughnuts, as pieces of jewelry, to finish an ensemble. It calls them an "original" gift. By some Byzantine logic, or illogic, it describes "doughnuts" as an American contraction of the English word *doughnut*, meaning "beignet," and that by extension the word *doughnut* means "ring-shaped" in "American"!

There are Malassada Beanie Babies and Krispy Kreme T-shirts, and Dreesen's has an enormous donut head mask for selling do-nuts on the street. The Bess Eaton chain had bags, cups, and boxes with evangelical mes-sages and signs.

Mark Isreal, donut innovator and owner of the Doughnut Plant, says, "I try to make the doughnut glamorous. *Glamour* magazine came in and did an article, and Isaac Mizrahi came in and made a designer doughnut. He signed it 'Isaac Mizrahi,' with his signature. It says, 'Doughnut Plant Couture.' And it says, 'Valrhona Chocolate Accessorized with Fresh Roasted Pistachios.' "

DONUT STYLE OLD & NEW
Mother-daughter dresses used to be all the rage. Now it's Designer Donuts. Isaac Mizrahi lent his name to Doughnut Plant Couture.

DOUGHNUT PLANT COUTURE

DESIGNED BY ISAAC MIZRAHI EXCLUSIVELY FOR DOUGHNUT PLANT VALRHONA CHOCOLATE ACCESSORIZED WITH FRESH ROASTED PISTACHIOS

FROM STYLE TO ART

Donuts to wear, donuts as adornments, designer donuts — these are a "question of style," a "look," lending another dimension to a necklace, an outfit. They are what they are and they are donuts too, and that lends them their whimsy and resonance. They are eye-catching because of their visual appeal, and also because of their allusive references, their stories. If it's a donut and at the same time not a donut, or more than a donut, it gets a double take or a laugh. At the other end of the donut-as-style/art continuum is the donut as subject of painting or photography by artists in the classical, high art tradition. And while donuts are morphing, they find forms to take — jewelry boxes, a window installation — that are somewhere between these categories.

When does an object used for another purpose, a donut-shaped box for storing jewelry, leave off being a tool or a craft and become a work of art? How do we classify a window installation featuring donuts that showcases the paintings in an art gallery while it looks like a work of art itself? As commerce? As décor? As art? Both the boxes and the window are more than utilitarian objects or advertising, and they are not merely stylish or faddish. Are the definitions of *art* and *style* in the eye of the beholder, or in the words of the critics, or in location? If it is in a window, does that mean it is not qualified to be in a museum?

As we are pondering these mysteries, there are some wonderful donuts to look at and get to know better.

I am taking an impromptu walk in Faneuil Hall Marketplace in Boston on one rainy Saturday night. In a gallery window I see a whole wall of shiny plates with gleaming chocolate brown plastic donuts on them. It shines into the wet night. Donuts. How did

they get there? What are they doing there? Are they art? Donuts, just when I am thinking donuts. Donuts-are-everywhere department. Later I call the Kennedy Gallery. It's a window, they say, not an art installation. The window designer is Kristin Lauer.

I find her and she says, "I just like fake food, I don't know." (This is surely one of the best lines I've heard.) "There's something

Kristin Lauer created this window installation of plastic chocolate donuts on plates for the Kennedy Gallery of Art in Boston.

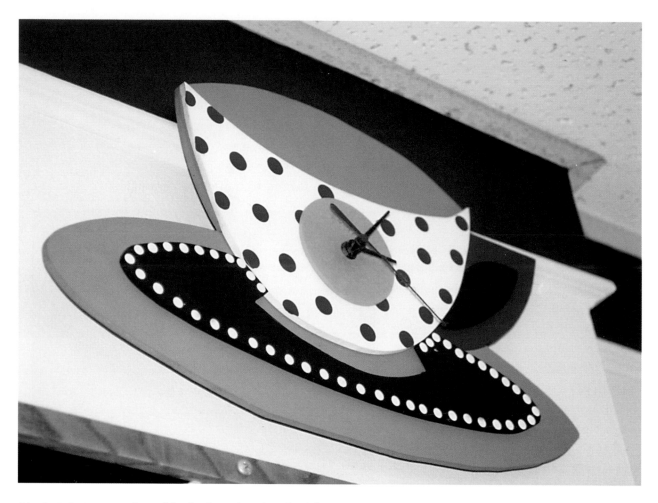

This clock is from one of America's most famous small donut shops, Coffee An' Donuts in Westport, Conn.

about fake food — I love it. I don't know why. But I really love it, like I loved Barbie dolls when I was seven. I don't know what it is — I think it's the plastic and the smell of it. It's weird. It's very satisfying."

There are the physical properties of the object, and then there are the meanings and associations of the image. "I like to use something that has a bit of retro chic to it, and is

kind of a pop culture symbol. Right now, it's a very cool and trendy thing, the donut," Kristin says. I ask how the donuts got into that window. She says it's the "gig" she has with Sullivan Properties in the Marketplace Center. They give her a space, lighting, and an assignment and then "they cut me loose in a storefront to do pretty much whatever I please. They wanted to support Kennedy

Gallery, which sells prints, so I found prints that were interesting. One was Damien Hirst's *Acid Tabs,* which is all circles, so I decided to do something three-dimensional that related to it."

She continues, "In terms of audience, the marketplace crosses all classes, cultures, ethnicities, and nationalities. People visit from all over the world. I was looking for a symbol that people would react to with some sort of fond familiarity, that would make them smile. Also kid-friendly is very important." There it is — donuts make people happy. She says, and this is important, "Then it's just its shape. I am interested in the fact that it is circular, and that it looked good inside of another circle."

Her comments on flavor choice: "I decided to go with chococlate because I liked the dark brown. Strawberry frosting was also available, but there wasn't enough contrast to the plate. It was too silly; I wanted it to be a bit more serious and less fake."

Kristin credits her midwestern origins with some of her inspiration: "I'm from Ohio. There's something about food and diners and kitsch that is instilled from my younger years. I do have a fascination with midwestern iconography, the whole Corn Belt thing. I have happy memories of growing up in a place where there were donut shops. I'm intrigued by the signage and the smell of them . . . I'm from Akron. Goodyear, Firestone, everything's a circle."

Tires, donuts, same thing.

She adds, "These days there's a blurring between commercial and fine art, thanks to Andy Warhol. People understand that commodity and commerce can be treated in that interesting sort of way." She specializes in surprise and invention. Kristin says that humor is important, the unexpected element. And that when you see something and don't know whether it's real or fake, "it adds a humorous grin to the piece. The donuts — I don't know — it really was right. I can tell by the smear marks on the glass. They are always about four feet high, smears and licks and stuff all over the glass — Yeah, smears!!!! . . . I can tell that the kids are running up to it and throwing themselves at it."

And the ultimate on fake donuts: "I really have kept my eye on these fake foods, I've been watching their evolution. For a while the Dunkin' Donuts label manufactured fake donuts and sold them at Toys 'R' Us, in the trademark orange-and-pink packaging. The great thing was they actually smelled like strawberry. Like really heinous strawberry air freshener. They're not around anymore. I've looked and looked. I put them out on a plate at a party I had and I kept watching people pick them up, but people stole them. I am very sad they're gone.

"The fake foods are all plastic but these were SCENTED, so that's very important to understand."

CHINESE DONUT BOXES

Just after looking at donuts plopping out of the machine in the window of McDonald's in Times Square, I am walking by a café on the Upper East Side. There in the window is a row of three shiny painted boxes with gold dragons on them, and they are shaped like oversize donuts. Donuts again and again, I think, as I go from the machine spilling out donuts for the masses in the interest of profit to boxes shaped like donuts created by artists. I go in, and a saleswoman says that the wife of the owner collects and sells these "Chinese Donut Boxes," made for jewelry.

So I look them up. Stefano Mazzieri wrote on the Internet, "I purchased an unusual donut-shaped wooden box in Guanzhou last year. I have since seen a similar box pictured in a book about Chinese artifacts. It is called a chaozhu and was used to hold the court necklace during the Qing dynasty, which was 1644–1911."

Then I call Patricia Attoe, the box importer and wife of the café owner. She tells me that her first encounter was in Macao, that she was looking for "interesting-shaped boxes and I fell in love with the shape." (The shape again, and another proof that the shape draws people for irrational reasons.) "I hadn't seen it anywhere, and I just thought it was very charming and I thought it was masculine enough to make a nice box for a man for cuff links or on a desk for stamps. Then I picked up a book called *True to Form*, which is about the art of Chinese crafts . . . I got it at the Mandarin Hotel walking through the lobby. The book caught my eye because the cover is an antique Donut Box."

Attoe's background is in art history, teaching art to young children. She wanted to do something of her own, and she loved travel and the creations of artisans in different parts of the world. She wanted to bring back their "goodies." Her husband owns the shop, RSVP, and he lets her use the window. She says that the friend she travels with was in Hong Kong, and Attoe thought it was a great place to start a business. "I love experiencing these different countries and the people and the food and the cultures. I've done well with the Donut Boxes."

Then the matter of shape comes up here too, that ultimate draw of the donut in all spheres — style or science, art or antiques,

These wood-and-lacquer Chinese donut boxes were made to hold jewelry in the Qing dynasty.

Martin Parr,
Common Sense,
1998.

whether to eat or to wear or to paint or to hold jewelry or to describe the universe. Echoing Lauer's thought that "then it's just their shape," Attoe says, "People buy it because they like the shape. I was emotionally attracted to it. I was drawn to it. I got very excited when I saw this box. I couldn't have said why. It was just emotional. I wanted to touch it. There was a certain comfort there. It spoke to me. There's something very sensual about roundness; you can take it all into the body form. There are two schools. There are people who like angular and those who prefer the round. I'm in the round camp, lots of curves, lots of roundness."

DONUTS IN AND AS ART

Donuts are in and as art, donuts as images and conceptualizations, rather than as food or things alone. They are showing up in the world of fine art, not just popular culture.

A donut can wink or beckon or invite. There is no end to the ways of looking at the donut, conceptualizing the donut, inventing the donut, designing the donut, personifying the donut, fashioning, creating the donut, interviewing the donut, romancing the donut, experiencing the donut.

"Donuts. Is there anything they can't do?" Bart Simpson asks.

Emily Eveleth, *high art explorations of the donut*

Emily Eveleth, painter of exquisite works in the tradition of the highest art, transforms donuts into artistic monuments in her paintings. They become quintessences, not only of themselves but also of light and form and shape, in her renowned paintings of donuts bathed in unearthly luminescence, in all their aesthetic wonder and beatitude. The paintings have appeared in the top galleries of New York and of the rest of the country. Her painting of a jelly donut was featured in *Gourmet* magazine, which calls her donuts "lush nudes . . . rendered in exquisite detail, their luminous flesh close enough to touch." Her donuts were also featured in a Zippy cartoon — "If the doughnuts of Emily Eveleth met the apples of Paul Cézanne would they fritter away their time discussing the holeness of th'universe?"

When you first see an Eveleth donut painting, the effect is riveting. The paintings are stunningly beautiful. Donuts never looked so good. Then comes the thought, Are these really paintings of donuts, that common food we eat without thinking? The real subject is something else altogether, something that is the subject of still life paintings through the ages — that is, art itself. Eveleth's paintings are not narrowly subject-driven. They result from a unique angle of vision, the flux between the observing eye, the painting hand, and the material inspiration. Beyond material and comestible, the donut is lifted from its physical life to exist as a conceptualization of a physical reality, a focus for the unique point of view and talent of a particular artist. The choice of something ordinary, perishable, taken for granted, is a starting point for a leap into another realm.

Eveleth says of her choice of donuts, "I'd put one, among other objects, in a painting.

"With a soft painterly touch, Ms. Eveleth turns humble jelly doughnuts into monumental, voluptuous objects of desire. Glowing and looming against dark backgrounds singly or in piled groups, they laze like corpulent odalisques. Each has its dark, raspberry-stained orifice turned to the viewer, to slightly alarming effect."
— Ken Johnson, in the *New York Times*

". . . it makes no more sense to think of Eveleth's doughnuts as doughnuts, period, than it does to think of Cézanne's apples as simply fruit."
— Robert Evans

And while I was making that painting, I recognized the potential of a doughnut as subject matter, for both its form and its associations."

About her work Eveleth says, "The appeal of painting doughnuts is a complicated thing. What first attracted me was the irony inherent in presenting them as monumental, painted images. But there's much more than that. Closely examined they are striking objects, with craggy convoluted forms, beautiful color and a glossy, oozing lusciousness. As icons of American consumer culture they are both omnipresent (for what else do you find stand-alone stores, open 24 hours?) and somehow slightly ridiculous. In presenting doughnuts as a painted image, in a monumental, heroic way, mediated through the language of paint and art history, a tension is created between what they are, with their associations with

Bluff, 2002, oil on canvas, 82 x 72 inches.

popular culture, and the elevation objects acquire through being painted in a serious manner. The paintings become something altogether new, something that I've never quite been able to define."

Five

DONUTS ARE U.S.

As I flew over America, I could see every crease and pleat of this country. I could see the plains, where I knew the sprays of wheat stretched golden, bending and nodding in the wind. We flew over the Grand Canyon and saw the cuts wind and water had made, turning the rock basin into a den of monsters and sphinxes. A mist like fine muslin hung over the necklace of jade green mountains dropping to the Pacific.

I came to appreciate the Americanness of Middle America when I lived there, to understand America in a way that is impossible if one lives on the edge. I learned its wilderness of towns and main streets with banks and real estate offices, its stretches of flat country baking in August, green grass singed yellow at the edges, the leaves of cornstalks flapping in the wind. At the edges of town there were strips, neon signs in large red and yellow letters marking supermarkets and discount stores, burger heavens and gas stations and movie houses, and donut shops.

Salvation Army women made donuts for soldiers in World War I. They were the rave of the trenches.

The donut flourishes in this American townscape. In this place, I thought of the origins of my grandfather in the vastness of this territory, his immersion in Americanness. He came from the America where I felt strange, an outsider. He knew what the real America would want, in its jungle of confetti-colored plastic and neon fighting for the attention of the parade of cars that continues toward the fields of grain and into the future.

Only in America, a land of initials where we forget the names, could DDU stand for Dunkin' Donuts University, a place where people who dream about donuts can make the dream come true. Only in America could donuts star on TV or become the subject of a business school course, showing how businesses go from farm to factory to street corner. In America, there are donuts at sukkah-building parties for the Jewish fall harvest festival, when people in skullcaps build booths with gourds and boughs to commemorate the wandering of the Jews. The writer Joan Didion speaks of the American woman's dilemma as she faces eating alone at night as a choice between "humiliation in a restaurant and 'eating a doughnut' in her hotel room." In no other country would that description be appropriate.

THE ORIGINAL SALVATION ARMY DONUT GIRL

I never expected to be in the Salvation Army headquarters, but there I was, carrying my copy of *Marching to Glory,* a history of the Salvation Army, next to people in blue uniforms with red shields, past the READ YOUR BIBLE EVERY DAY sign. Someone immediately asked, "What are you doing with that book?" I must have looked out of place. I explained and in answer I heard a story about how the Salvation Army gives an annual Golden Doughnut Award, a solid gold-covered ceramic donut for public service. After the Salvation Army made donuts the popular wartime food in World War I, the donut came to symbolize the good works of the Salvation Army. In the book I was carrying it says, "The winsome attractive coquetries of the round brown doughnut . . . practically eclipsed the rest of the Army's welfare service . . . With a stroke the Army's reputation was made." So important was the donut to the war works of the Salvation Army that the misconception arose that the Salvation Army had begun in France as a donut-making crusade.

Later I saw one of the awards in the cottage of Stella Young, the original Doughnut Girl of World War I. Postcards of the day featured a picture of her carrying a pan of donuts to soldiers outside the Salvation Army tent in wartime France. She appears in steel helmet and khaki uniform on the cover of the sheet music for a famous song from the war, "My Doughnut Girl." She spent her retirement living among the amusement parks and sandwich shops of Old Orchard Beach, Maine, in the area surrounding the Salvation Army headquarters. Nearby is its green shingle

At home the Salvation Army made donuts for immigrants arriving at Ellis Island.

Stella Young's Salvation Army Donuts

Here's an authentic recipe for the Salvation Army donuts the doughboys loved. *Makes about 3 dozen donuts*

    5 cups flour
    2 cups granulated sugar
    5 teaspoons baking powder
    ½ teaspoon salt
    2 eggs
    1¾ cups milk
    1 tablespoon lard
       Fat for deep frying
       Powdered sugar

Donuts must be thoroughly kneaded, rolled smooth, and cut into rings a little less than ¼ inch thick. Drop rings into fat that is hot enough to bubble when donut is dropped in. Turn donuts several times so they will brown evenly. Then lift them out, holding them over kettle a moment to drip. Dust with powdered sugar while hot.

tabernacle and outdoor meeting shell with the inscription GOD'S PROMISES ARE SURE IF YOU BELIEVE.

She told of being sent secretly on a boat to France at the age of 17. The seas were so violent that they thought the boat might sink. They made it to the tent at the front near a war-torn town, where they had few provisions. Then came the great rain, more than 30 days of it. One day, as the soldiers crowded around the Victrola, trying to cheer up, their nostalgia for home cooking led to the idea for the famous donuts. A chant arose, "We want donuts." Soon the Salvation Army women had filled a garbage pail with oil and made dough out of leftover flour, sugar, milk, water (carried by hand from the town pump in pails), baking powder, and vanilla. They used a wine bottle as a rolling pin and a seven-pound shell fitted with a one-pound shell to cut out donuts with holes.

Soon 500 soldiers stood waiting knee-deep in the muck outside the tent for the sweet fried mementos of home and hearth, of all things warm and wonderful. Eventually the women — or Sallies, as they were called — made 9,000 donuts in a day, with night shifts, the first around-the-clock donut shop in the tent among the muddy ruts filled with rain.

Word spread to other Salvation Army tents, and the Sallies started to make donuts wherever the war was being fought. Aviators dropped notes from planes saying they wanted donuts, dropped buckets from planes, lifted the donuts, and flew away.

Stella kept her steel helmet and the piece of shrapnel that hit the donut pan one day but just missed her as she was frying donuts. "If this were not here," she said, "I would not be here." There is a square in Boston named after her, Brigadier Stella Young Square. The donut appeared in parades like the one in Shreveport, Louisiana, where a float with a big donut said, "Salvation Army, Just a Reminder." In a commemorative exhibit in Philadelphia in 1926, an artist, asked to depict the Army for the city's sesquicentennial, sketched a huge Salvation Army lass holding a donut. It was not just the donuts, "bad as they were," said Stella, but what they did for the soldiers' morale that linked the good works of the Army with the donut. The donut and its spirit produced a song, which ends with these words:

> But of all the folks that mixed up
> In that beastly bloody swirl
> I cannot forget the graces
> Of the Little Doughnut Girl.

So in this way the donut became the symbol of the Army, and the Army started the donut on its way toward becoming an American symbol. The *New York Times* said, "When the memoirs of this war come to be written, the doughnuts . . . of the Salvation Army are going to take their place in history."

Soldiers frying donuts in garbage pails in World War I.

FROM HOLY TO HOLE-Y

In 1971 Peter Green, a Discalced Carmelite friar, left the monastery in upstate New York. He and his future wife, Jean, left in a 1957 pickup truck they had bought for $275. Jean had grown up in Michigan, had converted to Catholicism, and had become a "spiritual seeker," which had led her to the monastery.

They put some bolognas in the truck and headed south to form a "contemplative community of two." They stopped at the end of a red clay road in Columbia, Virginia, where they rented an unheated farmhouse on 200 acres of land for $30 a month. A short time later, they hit upon the idea of making ends

There ... a lady named Joan ... o said. "I'll dunk only at home!" (She meant it, too!)

Joan Bennett believes in a little, casual dunking, so it must be all right

Barrymore the Immaculate, Barrymore the Intense ... dunks with an air of deepest concentration

Above, expert dunkers Mary Brian, Gail Patrick and Dotty Lamour

One cup? Must be that Joel McCrea and Barbara Stanwyck believe in group dunking

DUNK DUNK DUNK NK

It could only happen in America. Nowhere else would such a lowly piece of dough have had a chance. Here, by virtue of its homely countenance, its meek submission to chronic dunkers, its unique adaptability to screwball publicity, this chunk of dough, the "sinker," has achieved heady, glorious heights ... Gag men for top radio comics — Burns and Allen, Eddie Cantor, Jimmy Durante, etc. — are dusting off ancient "dunking" jokes; 100 women's radio programs are running donut recipe contests ... Tin Pan Alley is knocking out a "Donut Song"; fashion will feature a "donut brown" material; Arthur Murray will teach a "donut hop."

Forbes magazine in 1949 noted the uniquely American quality of the donut in a "Sinker Saga."

meet by selling their own homemade donuts. Jean said, "Everyone will eat a donut. Besides, who says donuts are not spiritual? The way donuts rise is like incarnation." When he was reading the Revelations of Juliana of Norwich, a medieval English mystic, Peter came across the word *anchor-hold*, meaning hermitage, from the Greek for anchorite, hermit. They called their farm Anchorhold and asked, "What about Anchorhold donuts?" Peter and Jean said it was a difficult word for rural southerners, but that didn't stop them from buying Anchorhold donuts more often than other donuts. They bought them in grocery stores like Mrs. Dickinson's General Store, which Mrs. Dickinson ran with her 100-year-old mother, who was not sure which of her three or four husbands was which.

The Greens had no training for baking donuts. Leading up to his baking career, Peter had followed the contemplative life of the order of Discalced Carmelites, with their emphasis on deep inner prayer and on the simple life, symbolized by their sandals. *Discalced* means "unshod," so Peter had taken off his shoes for sandals. It was his reading of the life of Teresa of Ávila at the age of 29 that had sent him to the monastery, after a Catholic boyhood including parochial school, football, the Army, and even a stab at a Ph.D. The Carmelites sent him to the fishing villages of the Philippines, where he worked and trained new men for the order.

Peter and Jean made everything from scratch. With the carpentry learned from her father, Jean installed a $35 cast-iron stove, which they stoked with leftover wood from a sawmill. They built a chapel with an altar made of a telephone spool covered with a white cloth. There they offered mass, for themselves. "The donuts," they said, "were a little hard on the spiritual community."

On Mondays, when they went to Richmond for ingredients, they had their only free time — to eat sweet potato pie, or to get married, which they did one Monday in Goochland, Virginia. With the help of Pearl, "a big black woman who knew how to heft a 100-pound bag of glaze onto her shoulder," they managed to get their supplies onto the truck and take them home. Now they were in business, making 32 dozen Anchorhold donuts a day.

It was a hard life, 25 minutes of mixing by hand, living next to the baking room in the winter, since there was no heat. But they got to watch their donuts do "that marvelous thing they do when you put them in the fat, like a flower opening up." This section of Appalachia is a depressed area, people get by cutting pulpwood for the railroad. In spite of that, the Greens sold every donut they made — at Mrs. Dickinson's, and in Fork Union, where the 600 boys at the military school ate fourteen dozen a day. "Wow, that's what saved us!" the Greens said.

STAN STAN THE DONUT MAN

Stanley Aloysius Andersen began his career on the streets of Jersey City elbowing his way through the crowds selling "polish" and ended up as Stan Stan the Donut Man. He passed out so many donuts in World War II that FDR gave him a Distinguished Service Medal even though he never fought in a battle.

The son of a Norwegian dockworker and a "New York gal," Stanley had a withered hand that people wouldn't let him forget. He quit school at 14. At 17 he hooked up with a Native American, Chief Black Hawk, or "Charlie," complete with a tomahawk, feathers, and a whole show's worth of trickery. They put together that old American pastime, the medicine show, selling snake oil, hair tonic, and herbs. They moved out to the towns of America, talking about life on the streets of New York.

Former snake-oil pitchman Stan Stan the Donut Man gave out donuts to the troops in World War II.

"So you want to go into the Donut Business ?"

Saturdays they would ride into a town square. Chief Black Hawk sang songs and told stories and did magic. Then Stanley got up on the stump and loosened up the crowd. He talked about snake oil and how it was made of roots and barks and berries that brought healing to the body. He promised a cure for anything. Snake oil, he said, was good for scalp itch, ingrown toenails, stiff joints. To show how it seeps into joints, he rubbed it into a piece of leather and the oil oozed through. Miraculous lubricating qualities. "You won't get me caught by the police, will you?" Stanley asked me. "Actually, we pricked the leather with a fine needle . . .

"The business of the medicine show was psychology, not medicine," said Stan the pitchman. "It was the psychology between me and the crowd that sold the product. It almost didn't matter what the product was. The people wanted entertainment and they got it."

Stan and the chief stayed together for four years. Then Stan's father died, so he knew he would need a better job. He answered an ad in the paper for selling donuts and donut machines in dime stores all over the country. When he walked into the office of the Doughnut Corporation of America, he knew this was just what he was looking for, and the men in the company knew he was just what they were looking for. "I had the guts to bark and ballyhoo about the donut the way I had with snake oil. I made donut shows the same

as I had made the medicine shows, and I found myself through donuts," said Stan.

Stan, like my grandfather, understood America's grassroots and small towns. Stan made everyone in every dime store in all those American towns notice donuts. The conviviality of donuts, he called it. Eat them and your fight with your spouse is done. He sold donuts from the stump, with his gift for hawking, a gift like speaking in tongues. He traipsed through plains and mesas, a donut hobo with donuts in his bandanna, roaming the country and tossing donuts the way Johnny Appleseed tossed seeds. He made up a name and a comic book personality for himself, so he could sell donuts, and he made it come alive. Stan Stan the Donut Man, he called himself, and so did everyone else, the 4-H Club kids and the drum majorettes, the soldiers and FDR, and the *New Yorker* writers who wrote about him. He made up a donut pitch, about donuts going back to the Bible, the donut as the Word of God made manifest on Earth.

Stanley made donuts famous as they were making him famous. Later, when he became secretary of the National Dunking Association of 3 million donut dunkers, he made up donut routines for Hollywood stars — Jimmy Durante and Lucille Ball getting laughs for donuts, Gracie Allen eating them with boxing gloves. Stanley sat around lobbies of hotels in New York to practice feeling comfortable with celebrities and rich people.

At the start of World War II, he wanted more than anything to be able to fight, because he felt the "fever that hits every man at the start of a war," and he knew he couldn't because of his hand. It was then that my grandfather gave him the job that made him famous throughout the country and the world. Stan Stan the Donut Man was known by every soldier in the war.

So Stan and my grandfather organized the donut campaign with a war donut pitch. My grandfather remembered the Salvation Army ladies and their donuts and loaned his machines to the Red Cross. He sold them mix at a low price so they could give away the donuts. He showed the Red Cross people how to use the machines, which he put on trucks he called Clubmobiles, with record players and Red Cross ladies to hand out donuts and dance with soldiers.

Stan's war routine was filled with wisecracks and donuts for "every Yank who captures a Jerry." He organized donut-eating contests for "chowhounds." But Stan's trademark was his challenge to soldiers to call out the name of their hometowns, and if he didn't know where the main streets and parking lots and altars were in a particular town, that soldier would get a box of donuts, and Stan

Lucille Ball enjoys donuts on the set.

Three classics — glazed, powdered sugar, and cruller.

would send five boxes to the soldier's family. Stan knew most of the towns from the oceans to the prairies, and he got the soldiers from those towns together with the town-name-calling routine. Donuts, he said, were a bridge to home. He had a gimmick for everything. If you called out, "Hey, Stan, how the hell are ya?" he would toss some donuts.

In Rome, Stan stood in the Piazza del Popolo and gave away 8,000 donuts a day. While machine guns were firing, Stan set up a nightclub and a barbershop for soldiers, all with donuts, and the men brought him fresh vegetables and eggs to eat, and so much wine that he lost his taste for it. From Saipan to Guadalcanal to Salerno and Iwo Jima, Stan narrowly missed sniper fire, going right to the front, helping the wounded, handling German prisoners even, giving donuts to soldiers who had no other "mess." The *New Yorker* called Stan's giving out donuts for the Red Cross "its most tangible form of therapy."

At one point, Stan got mad at the French, who were out on a Pacific island trying to make a profit in the war by selling French crullers to American troops for 48 cents a dozen. The Real American Donut, which the patented Wonderful Almost Human Automatic Donut Machine made for eight cents a dozen, was free for the soldiers. Stan hurried out to the Pacific to stop French oppression by donuts. Donuts, Stan had everyone saying, are sooooooo American. And Stan made

them so popular that many soldiers wrote queries to the U.S. government, which issued a booklet on how to go into the donut business, all because the soldiers wanted to do what Stan did so well.

And then Stan received a Distinguished Service Medal from President Franklin D. Roosevelt. He was one of very few civilians to receive this award. Stan got a medal for serving thousands of donuts to front-line troops, for service to the Red Cross, the soldiers, the war, America. "If only," he said, "we could have brought the Germans and Americans together around donuts."

DONUT DREAMS AT DDU

At Dunkin' Donuts University, I found a couple who had come from rural Pennsylvania after years of saving their money to make the dream of having their own donut shop come true. The American donut dream still lives for them and others like them who come with their own money to put into these donut shops. Donut dreamers come from Texas and Utah and Kentucky, and they all say that five weeks at DDU isn't quite enough for a donut education.

This couple are in their 50s. She was a substitute music teacher, he was a locksmith, and they gave up their jobs to buy a shop, to stray thousands of miles from home, to learn in the training kitchens of DDU, where everything is whitened with a coat of flour. In white apron and baker's hat with the Dunkin' Donuts logo in chubby, pink and orange donutlike letters, the music teacher and the locksmith are trying to roll out dough with oversize rolling pins. It's uneven. "Everything's so big, even the rolling pin. It's not like baking a pie at home," the wife says. They are nervous about their career change, but hopeful. The manager tells me, "They've got a lot to learn. Cake donuts today, yeast-raised tomorrow."

The sweet smell of donuts and the fog of flour make me feel that I am in a fragrant, cakey dream. Everywhere are bins and racks of donuts and donut holes, some in a card-board lunch box painted like wood with a handle. You can pay more for a glass apple filled with donut holes if you want them fancy.

Dunkin' Donuts was started by William Rosenberg in 1950, growing from a meal deliv-cry service to a coffee shop, the Open Kettle, outside of Boston, and then to the first Dunkin' Donuts shop in Quincy, Massachusetts. Now it has 52 kinds of donuts and 5,500 shops throughout the world, reaching from Boston to Curaçao and the Philippines.

DDU: At Dunkin' Donuts University, donut dreams come true. Future franchisees learn everything about donut selling and donut making.

ALWAYS USE PURE VERMONT MAPLE

CANDIED SWEET POTATOES
Cook six medium-sized sweet potatoes until tender. Peel and slice lengthwise. Cover with ¾ cup maple syrup, or maple sugar and dot with butter. Add ¼ cup water, salt and pepper. Bake about 35 minutes at 325°. Serves 6.

SHAKE UP A "VERMONTER"
¾ cup ice cold milk, 2 tbs. Vermont maple syrup. Scoop of vanilla ice cream. Shake well and serve. Serves one.

MIX A MAPLE SPECIAL
For sweetening, add at least 3 teaspoons of pure Vermont maple to your favorite fizz, Bacardi, Old Fashioned, Sour or other drink.

MAPLE SYRUP IS DELICIOUS:
on pancakes and waffles
on grapefruit — try it broiled
on hot cereal — warm syrup
on ice cream — cold syrup
on French toast — warm syrup
with baked apples
to sweeten custard pie
to sweeten egg nogs
to sweeten your favorite beverage
as a bedtime snack, heat glass of milk to 120° and add maple syrup to flavor
try 1 tbsp. Vermont maple syrup to 1 glass of ginger ale.

MAPLE BAKED HAM SLICE
With ham slice in shallow dish, pour on about ¼ cup maple syrup. Bake, if pre-cooked, 30-35 minutes in slow oven 325°. Some might like to use 1 tsp. dry mustard also. Try this and you'll never serve plain ham again.

THROW A "SUGAR ON SNOW" PARTY!
To prepare "Sugar on Snow" use large kettle with syrup less than one-fourth of kettle capacity. Butter the top edge of the kettle. Start with high heat but watch the pot without leaving. Turn heat down when syrup threatens to boil over. Several minutes later when the thermometer reach 230° take out a tablespoon full, cool it slightly over packed snow or crushed ice and pour it on snow or ice. If the poured liquid sugar clings in a lock as soft waxy taffy the batch is ready to serve. Before serving, cool the boiling liquid sugar in serving pitchers to below 190° but above 150°; pour it on snow or ice in narrow strips. A quantity of syrup will lose one-fifth of its volume in the boiling. Please don't eat the snow!

"SUGAR ON SNOW" for 35-40 persons (¼ + cup each): 1 gallon Vermont Maple Syrup, Fancy or Grade A, 1 bushel clean snow. Serve on snow packed tray. 4 doz. unsweetened donuts, 1 qt. sour pickles. Deviled eggs, milk, coffee.

Hoffman Photo

SUGAR SHACK
New England loves its maple-sugaring ritual, complete with its snack of donut, pickle, and "sugar on snow," all in one mouthful.

DONUT, PICKLE, AND SUGAR ON SNOW

Harry Morse doesn't always tell visitors at his Vermont Sugar Shack how to eat Sugar on Snow, or Sugar Eat, as the house offering is called. He says he assumes that if they came all the way to Montpelier, they must know what to do with it, but the truth is they don't. They don't know that you push a dollop of syrup onto a box of snow until it gets rubbery, then put it in your mouth at the same time that you take bites of garlic pickle and fresh, homemade donut. The combination is instant zing. The idea is that the pickle lessens the sweetness so that you can eat more sweet than you would otherwise. This ritual of donut, pickle, and Sugar on Snow goes back to Native American and Pilgrim times. The Morse family members were some of the oldest settlers up here. Today Mrs. Morse has made 500 donuts for the busloads.

Harry's voice is as rough as a New England winter, his face weathered tree bark, a voice from the woods, telling the lore of Native Americans and early settlers in this land of maple trees decked in carnival gear in the fall and dressed in buckets catching juices in spring. Harry says, "I was born on a kitchen table up the road. My father was a dairy farmer, and he only did sugaring in season, but I like it better, so I do it all year. In the summer we make the snow ourselves in the ice machine." He talks of seeing steam rising from the chimneys all over, and how people would invite others to come and eat "the fussings."

As we look over the blizzard blurring the white wooden church steeple and the bare black branches, like a Christmas card scene, Harry tells how his ancestors moved up to Vermont from southern New England and learned the sugar business from the Native Americans. There are legends about how the native people started making maple syrup in the woods, collecting the sap in scooped-out logs and boiling it down to syrup by dropping hot rocks into it. One legend says it was the temper tantrum of a brave who put his squaw's pot next to a tree and then let the tree have it with his ax. The next day the squaw took her pot full of liquid and put in some deer meat, not knowing she was making the first maple syrup until she tasted it.

When the Morse ancestors did their sugaring long ago, each family tapped a few trees

with handmade wooden spouts and filled wooden tubs with sugar. They carried buckets of sap on wooden yokes on their shoulders, like working bulls, and brought them to the open fire, to the kettle supported on a stick over a fire, where sap boiled. Then they celebrated with the early Sugar on Snow parties right in the snowdrifts, cooling the sugar until it had the rubbery feel of gooey candy. Later, people built sugarhouses in the woods with no electricity and moved into them for the sugaring season. The donut-and-pickle accompaniment to Sugar on Snow has been part of the celebration for generations.

"Did you know that each sugar bush has a slightly different taste, and the syrup that comes from it is different too?" Harry asks. Mrs. Morse got her donut recipe from a newspaper, and she says if you fry them, they're donuts and if you bake them, they're rolls. As Harry Morse says, "Donuts are so New England, it's a natural. But they have to be unsweetened donuts and fluffy to be good. And my wife says the snow has to be packed into the container for the sugar, and it isn't right unless you do it with your hands."

Today, tradition is mixed with modern technology in Harry Morse's Sugar Shack. He tells stories of tomahawks chopping down trees as he shows us the plastic tubes, used for intravenous feeding in hospitals, that link the trees and pour the sap into huge tanks. This sugar sucker hitches 1,000 trees, using vacuum power to suck sap from the sugar bush, as the trees together are called.

We go into the sugarhouse and it's all maple steam, like a sauna, and when people come in they get rid of their colds. The half-light makes it

Sugar on Snow

The traditional culinary accompaniment to "sugaring off" in New England, when maple trees are tapped for sap, is the unlikely combination of pickle, donut, and "sugar on snow," or maple syrup poured onto snow. This is a spring ritual in the woods. It tastes surprising, and surprisingly good, combining sweet and sour and cold and warm. The donut I had at Harry Morse's Sugar Shack was homemade by Mrs. Morse and was among the best donuts ever.

Vermont fancy grade A light amber maple syrup
Pure white snow
Sour pickles
Donuts

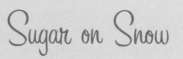

Heat the syrup to 255°F. Scoop the snow into a large bowl or pan. Drizzle hot maple syrup lightly over the snow. Use a fork to eat the sticky top layer. Follow with a bite of sour pickle and your favorite donut.

eerie and rustic. The smell of maple makes it a maple world. Then Harry shows us how to push the sugar onto the snow and eat it all at once — donut, pickle, and sugar, soft, sticky, crunchy textures, sweet and sour and doughy. It's hard to stop eating.

BEGORRA, HERE COMES MISTER DONUT

Patrick James O'Hanlon was born on March 12, and the parish priest insisted that his name follow Saint Patrick first, rather than his uncle Jim. This was not the way the family had chosen, so they called him Jim when he got back from church, to avoid annoyances. Born to a carpenter and his wife on a farm in County Armagh, Ireland, he was the only son, and the brother of four sisters. He was educated by tough Irish Christian brothers in a parochial day school and was walloped into learning before he started in real life as a grocer's apprentice, buying butter from country people, measuring sugar and flour. One dol-

Born in Ireland, Jim O'Hanlon went from rags to riches in a Mister Donut shop.

lar a week, two the next year, then three. No promise, no prospects.

After five years at the grocer's, he took up tilling on a farm. He was not cut out for it, so he put down the hoe and said, "Jim, it's time to move." He had no future in Ireland. He tried a job as a switchboard operator, briefly, and he met a nurse named Bess at Daisy Hill Hospital, County Down, but he couldn't afford to marry her. Finally, he spent all of his savings on passage to America and arrived with $2.25 in his pocket. A year later, Bess followed him to America. He got a job as an elevator operator at the Hotel McAlpin, Thirty-fourth Street and Herald Square, New York City, $32 a week, 32 years old. "It had its ups and downs," he says. A definition of upward mobility.

"It could only happen in this country," said Jim, "that I arrive with $2.25 in my pocket, no debts, and that now I owe $375,000 to the bank." This was decades later, after he became the most famous Mister Donut of the Mister Donut chain, with four donut shops in Delaware, a place he had to look up on a map when he went to start in donuts.

Jim said he would pick me up at the station in a two-tone Cadillac Seville. Up to that point, all I knew of him was that he was a donut shopkeeper. He said I would recognize him by his Irish cap. I did, and the brogue, and the red hair, and the blue eyes to go along. Not the usual tycoon, and not the usual donut man either.

Jim made it out of the elevator and into the restaurant at the McAlpin. He studied food and wine and became the wine steward. He went to school at night and lived in a third-floor walk-up with three kids on $64 a week. He went to work first at Luchow's restaurant, then at Patricia Murphy's Candlelight Restaurant in Yonkers, for $125 a week. He bought a TV in spite of his wife's objections. He wanted to go into business for himself. Still no prospects.

One night on TV he saw an ad for a start-your-own-business show in New York. He went to the show and looked around. His wife was hungry and made a beeline for the donut booth in the middle of the floor. She sat down and ate a lemon donut. It was a transforming experience. She called to her husband, "This is it, Jim." He said, "This is what?" She replied, "Have one." He did. It was good. She said, "This is the business for us." He thought, Never oppose a woman. He inquired about donuts. The only available opening in the company represented by the booth, Mister Donut, was in Wilmington, Delaware. He had never heard of it. He went down to Delaware to see a donut shop on the highway near a construction site and vacant lot. It didn't look promising, and he had already left the Land of No Promise. But his wife liked it. He sold his house and bought a franchise.

He had wondered if Wilmington would need an education about donuts. It didn't.

"They surprised the life out of me," he said. The first week he did $3,700 worth of business. The break-even point was $2,100. From then on he made money every day. "All you need is good coffee and donuts, and twenty hours a day," he said. Jim wore a white uniform, was a baker of donuts, a sweeper of floors, a busboy, at 45 years old: "I had a lot of butterflies." The shop's earnings rose to $10,000 a week. Jim got four shops, one by one, each in the top 10 of the hundreds of Mister Donut shops in the United States, one of them number one.

The *Virginia Pilot* wrote an article about him that said, "At 45 he entered success through a donut hole."

Jim said his stores were so crowded in the morning that people couldn't get in. He said the key was nickel-and-diming your way up. "Even if we charged ten dollars a donut, it would be a nickel-and-dime business, but with all the headaches of a big corporation. There's only one way to make a business succeed. It's the people," he said.

He bought his first ticket back to Ireland after 17 years, a first-class jet ticket. People said, "You lucky Irishman." He replied, "That's bunkum. I was out working while that guy was asleep." That year he was selling almost three million donuts a year.

A CLASSIC PAIR
Coffee and donuts are America!

SADIE, LOUISE, AND TED

I met Sadie Anzalone, donut packer, an Italian with the name Sadie. "What's your real name, Sadie?" I asked. "Sadie. Oh. My real name? Oh, Maria Rosaria." How did you get to be called Sadie?" "I grew up in a Jewish neighborhood. My girlfriend's mother, Mrs. Hoffman — I can see her now — she heard my grandma call me by the nickname of Serena, and she mistook it for Sadie, so ever since that day she called me Sadie, and so did everyone else. She said, 'Sadeh'le, come up,' and I used to eat the rye bread with the chicken fat." Sadie was 18 when she became one of America's first women donut packers. Her father, a barber, came to America from Sicily. "Wasn't this the land of opportunity?" she said. Sadie's mother sewed pea jackets for the Navy in the war, and Sadie packed donuts. The machinists sometimes stayed up all night, sending the donuts on Warmobiles, which rolled around American neighborhoods selling war bonds and giving free donuts to buyers. Sadie said, "Donuts were being remembered. We had a value in the war."

The people on the assembly line with Sadie were all "neighborhood people." She loved working there because of the group feeling. "The German guy stayed all night cleaning up and singing at the top of his lungs. It was exciting. People went bananas over the same donut in a different package," Sadie said.

Louise Doyle grew up in Maine, near loggers' camps. Louise was Italian. She was the valedictorian of her high school class, but she was too poor to go on in school. "The logging camps had these long tables that were filled all the time with donuts, and that's where we got them. My mother would never make them, she thought it was frivolous. Italians never ate donuts. We only saw donuts in the logging camps and in the houses of the Poles and the Finns. You know," she continued, "we could speak Polish and they could speak Italian, that's the way it was in Millinocket. Everyone understood each other, no matter what the words were. The Polish mama made these

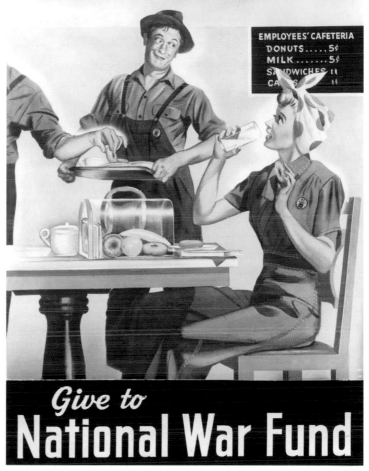

Zestful Nourishment

EMPLOYEES' CAFETERIA
DONUTS.....5¢
MILK.......5¢
SANDWICHES 1¢
CA S 1¢

Give to
National War Fund

donuts, they were yeast-raised, they were this high, they were so light they could walk away. Then the cooks in the logging camps learned to make them for the loggers. The assistants, the cook-ees, took out the holes. Then they cooked the holes. We got donuts for the first time in a donut shop that made the first Down

Warmobiles with free donuts for war-bond buyers rolled around American towns in World War II.

East Donut. They were just big and crunchy on the outside, no icing, and they were the only real sweets we had as kids."

Ted Andrews went east from his native South Dakota. His father had made a deal with the railroad to stop at a town he had laid out himself. The trains rumbled through and clanged to a stop in the place where winter snow came up to the second-story windows and you could walk right into the bedrooms. His father laid out another town that grew to 200. He went on to become the richest man in South Dakota.

Ted went east because he thought he was too smart for that little town. He saw a donut machine in a window, bought it and part of a barrel of flour. Later he said they were the making of his bakery. Within a year he had put the two bakers next to him out of business with the donuts from the machine. He had the second largest bakery in New England. Then he took the machine to Old Orchard Beach, Maine, where it was the craze of the beach that summer, in the early 1920s. People wanted to know where to get the miraculous machine. He ended up selling machines all over America for my grandfather's donut company.

THEN AND NOW
An early Krispy Kreme shop is as crowded as one today.

Orange Sour Cream Donuts

A bite of these cakey donuts reveal a hint of orange and the tang of sour cream. When served hot on a chilly morning, they are a sweet way to start the day. Adapted from *U.S.A. Cookbook* by Sheila Lukins. *Makes 28 donuts and holes*

2 large eggs
1 cup granulated sugar
¾ cup sour cream
¼ cup milk
3 tablespoons unsalted butter, melted
1 tablespoon orange marmalade, melted
2 teaspoons finely grated orange zest
3⅓ cups all-purpose flour
1 tablespoon baking powder
1 teaspoon salt
½ teaspoon ground nutmeg
Vegetable oil, for frying
Confectioners' sugar, for dusting
(optional)

1. Whisk the eggs in a large bowl until light and lemon-colored. Gradually add the granulated sugar, whisking constantly until the mixture is thick and ribbony.

2. Stir in the sour cream, milk, melted butter, melted marmalade, and orange zest.

3. In another bowl, sift the flour, baking powder, salt, and nutmeg together. Add this to the egg mixture, and stir to combine. Do not overwork the dough. Let the dough rest in the refrigerator for 20 minutes.

4. Pour oil to a depth of 2 to 3 inches in a large, heavy pot, and place it over medium-high heat. Heat it to a temperature of 370°F.

5. While the oil is heating, roll the dough out on a lightly floured surface to about ¼-inch thickness. Using a floured 2½ inch donut or biscuit cutter, cut it into rounds. (If you don't have a donut cutter, cut out the center holes with an apple corer. Save the holes!

6. When the oil has reached 370°F, fry the donuts in small batches until golden brown, turning once, 1½ minutes per side. It's best to stand back and wear a long-sleeved shirt or chef's jacket to prevent burns from splashing oil. Use a slotted spoon to remove them from the oil, and set them on paper towels to drain. Then fry the donut holes (they'll take about 30 seconds per side). Watch the temperature of the oil; let it reheat between batches if necessary.

7. Sprinkle the donuts with confectioners' sugar, if desired, and serve warm.

Six

Tales from the
DONUT TRAIL

The donut is a piece of Americana. It is our cultural artifact, although it may be part of all other societies at holiday times. It is in America that donuts are associated with wars and cops and churches, with the *Mayflower* and the machine and the open road. They are part of American social history, its places and pastimes and popular culture. "I want me a blueberry donut," the guy says on the TV news.

People are nuts, so to speak, about good donuts, which get the kind of attention as a food icon that, say, sticky buns and coffee cake do not. It's not just that the donut can relieve the sugar low that comes in the late afternoon as a result of biorhythms common to humanity at large, giving rise to afternoon teas as well as coffee breaks. The eating of this ring-shaped cake has behind it the whole of human history and its gravitation to circles and to circular foods.

Scott Livengood, CEO of Krispy Kreme, says, "If there wasn't a hole, it wouldn't be a doughnut. The nothingness of the center creates the somethingness of the doughnut."

Donuts appeal to something so fundamental in human nature that it defies analysis. It just is. As far back in time as we can go, even before the mention of donuts in the Bible, maybe cavemen ate donuts . . . Below is a visual aid from a street in Barcelona. Simian donuts? Hominid donuts?

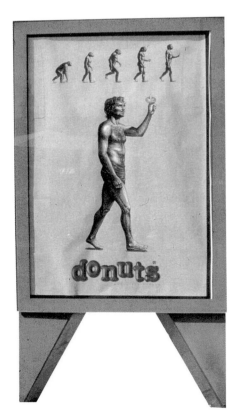

Donuts eternal, donuts American, from caveman donuts to American "Yankee" donuts, above, with blueberry stripes.

HOW TO MAKE AN AMERICAN DONUT

I am sitting at the bar at Craft restaurant, an elegant New York eatery where the pastry chef has created a fancy donut for dessert. Donuts are an American craft. They give off vibes of America and soldiers and truck stops and the prairie and city streets, and when you eat one, even if it is in an elegant restaurant, it still carries with it the baggage of its associations and connotations, and that makes it even better than a rogue creation by an inventive chef. Calling it a donut lifts it into an image, a comestible with a history and a story and with all the experience of donut eating behind it. However they taste, these are donuts.

Under the rustic/modern décor with lots of wood and terra-cotta, the food at Craft is made of high-quality ingredients presented in all their superb simplicity, combined into a meal by the diner. The meal is "crafted" by you, the patron.

These donuts are cinnamon sugar and chocolate. They are made of brioche dough, the latest fad in fancy donut making, which makes them light and buttery, not heavy with fat. They are airy nothings — well, almost. They don't have heft but they have so much delicacy and flavor that they end up being intense but ethereal. The shape is inventive: There is no hole, but rather a dent in the middle where a small knob, maybe even a "nut" of dough, the "hole," sticks up and says hi, tipping its hat. The chocolate is the best chocolate icing you've ever had on the best chocolate "donut" you've ever had.

Next to me is a couple, also eating donuts. The man tells me the story of the cider donuts he grew up with in Vermont, the best — well, next to these — he says. That's the thing about donuts. You encounter one or talk about one, and then you are hearing everybody's donut story. Donuts are everywhere and everything to everyone. They are art, and craft, and recipes, snacks, and metaphors to all the donut-eating folks of the world.

ANTHROPOLOGY OF DONUTS

There is a real anthropology/ethnography of donuts — all the nationalities with their do-nuts and all the people in America who work with donuts, Greek, Hawaiian, Cambodian, Polish, Jamaican. Cambodians abound in donut shops in California, owning the lion's share of shops there in the state that has the

Life's simple pleasures: donuts and a smile.

greatest number of donut shops per capita in the United States. Some of the Cambodian refugees learned the names of donuts as their first English words and donut making as the first thing they did in America.

There's a Dunkin' Donuts shop in Zamboanga, the Philippines, which set a record for donut sales. It is a hot spot at night and at afternoon snack time in this unlikely donut outpost.

In Israel, donuts, called *sufganiyot*, are well-known Hanukkah delights, especially popular among black-coated Hasidic Jews, who line up to get them. One year there was a "sufganiya war," in which political parties handed out propaganda and documents, like Israel's Declaration of Independence, with the donuts, to make a point.

Does the idea of Saudi donuts seem like a stretch? A 2002 article on the front page of the *New York Times* about Arab boycotts of American goods begins, "Doughnuts may not be quite as American as, say, apple pie, but they come close enough to make Samir Nasier, a Saudi fast-food king, nervous." And then, "Mr. Nasier [muses] aloud that doughnuts might qualify as traditional Saudi fare, given that he started making them 21 years ago."

Jonah, an anthropologist, and his wife, Emily, a linguistics student, are eating a sweet potato donut at the Cupcake Café in New York. They are about to go to Tajikistan to study the Ismaili sect.

In Tajikistan, Emily and Jonah see a Tajik dessert that is a kind of donut, a crisp, fried, flaky pastry, a confection of concentric rings with a hole and powdered sugar for dipping into tea. It's called *salla* in Tajiki. They tell me that the Turkish restaurant in Dushanbe has a menu called Donuts — cheese donut, sesame donut, soft donut, filled donut.

Menu of donuts in Tajikistan, some sweet, some savory.

DONUT TALK AT THE CUPCAKE CAFÉ

New York's Cupcake Café makes some of the best donuts in the city.

Mike and Ann Warren own the Cupcake Café, near the Port Authority Bus Terminal, at 39th Street and 9th Avenue in New York City. The shop is unassuming, with a hand-painted sign like a kid's art project. But it gets everybody, from suburban wives to Upper East Side ladies to theater types to bus drivers down from Harlem. The chairs are cracked; the place is not fancy. It's plain, seedy even, but in the glass cases, there are the puffy donuts, Sweet Potato and Dunky Oaty and Whole Wheat Orange, dripping with curtains of white glaze.

A guy buying a donut says, "I'm not a big fan of topping. Orange sounds good. Whole wheat orange." Everyone wants donuts. The Malaysian guy with gold bangles in his ears, the coffee-colored bus driver, the blond woman with the dog who says the rhubarb pie reminds her of the rhubarb in her childhood garden. She's wearing a red, white, and blue pin in the shape of an apple, with stars and stripes across it, rhinestone stars sparkling.

In one of the display cases, there's a package of Doughnut Seeds, Cakus Selectus Yummy.

The Warrens started in 1988. "We tried five million recipes," Ann says. "We make our own donuts from scratch. Six kinds of donuts. We fried them in our apartment. I learned a lot about making donuts making donuts."

"Hey," she says, "if it's not fried, it's not a donut."

Mike says, "We started out of desperation. My wife the brain invented it."

Howard the retired bus driver is eating the fattest glazed donut cut in pieces. He came all the way from uptown for these donuts.

They are moistened with sweet potato and made from scratch. He cleans the crumbs off the table meticulously. The donuts have an orange glow to them from the sweet potato.

He says, "Excellent, yes! I came from all the way uptown, excellent yes. Better than Krispy Kreme and all that. This you can't even touch. I come in here. I was born in Virginia." He says this in a southern accent. "Norfolk. I live in New York most of my life. I've been a bus driver for the city for twenty years. Sweet potato glazed! Hmmm, delicious."

Ann says, "We liked donuts well enough, but it wasn't like we were completely donut-crazy. There just weren't any good donuts available."

Mike says to me, "You coming back at 3 A.M. when we fry?"

Dunky Oaty Doughnuts

Ann and Mike Warren, owners of New York's Cupcake Café, maintain that donuts can be healthy. Here's one of their contributions to the growing arsenal of donuts as health food. These have whole grains, walnuts, honey, buttermilk, and even wheat germ in them.

Makes about 1 dozen doughnuts

2½ cups whole wheat flour

2 cups unbleached flour

1 tablespoon plus 1 teaspoon baking powder

2 teaspoons cinnamon

1½ teaspoons baking soda

1⅓ teaspoons salt

½ teaspoon mace

1⅔ cups rolled oats

1 cup chopped walnuts, medium fine

½ cup wheat germ

6 eggs

2 cups buttermilk

1 cup light brown sugar

⅓ cup honey

2 ounces melted butter (¼ cup)

1 teaspoon lemon zest

¾ pound solid vegetable shortening per quart fryer capacity (for a 4-quart fryer, use 3 pounds shortening)

Confectioners' sugar for dusting (optional)

1. Sift together the flours, baking powder, cinnamon, baking soda, salt, and mace. Add the oats, walnuts, and wheat germ. Combine well and put aside. Combine the eggs, buttermilk, brown sugar, honey, butter, and zest and add to the dry mixture. Do not overmix. Chill in refrigerator for 30 minutes to 1 hour to make handling easier.

2. When the dough is not too soft or sticky, it is ready to roll on a floured board. You can use bran or whole wheat flour to flour the board if you like. Roll the dough to ¾ to 1 inch thick and cut rings using a doughnut cutter or two biscuit cutters — first a larger one (2½ to 3 inches in diameter), then, inside that, a smaller one (about 1¼ inches).

3. Meanwhile, gradually heat up shortening to about 365°F — not beyond. Fry four or five doughnuts at a time for about 2 minutes on each side. Remove and place on absorbent paper (such as paper towels) to drain. Sprinkle doughnut with confectioners' sugar, if using, when cooled slightly.

Ann says, "Foolishly enough, they are actually measured from scratch every day.

"My favorite is the whole wheat oatmeal donut. We based our whole wheat donut on the Chock Full O' Nuts Whole Wheat Donut."

I ask, "Is it true that celebrities come in here?"

"So I've been told," Ann replies, "but I'm one of the worst sighters. Garrison Keillor came in and I never even saw." Mick Jagger, Barbra Streisand, and Madonna have all made appearances.

Mike says, "My wife is in love with your grandfather. She wants a machine in our window over there because it's so close to where your grandfather's first shop on 42nd Street was."

To the clientele at large, Mike says, "This lady's grandfather invented the donut machine."

The round proud donuts sell out by closing time, 7 P.M.

BIBLICAL DONUTS, HOLY MESSENGERS

Bess Eaton was a New England bakery chain known for its donuts and for the scriptural messages on its cups and boxes. All the packaging was red, white, and blue, and said BESS EATON, with the *o* as a heart, sometimes with a cross inside it, and with the saying, "Christ † Is The Answer." Some of it also had LOVE, JOY, PEACE, PATIENCE, GOODNESS, KINDNESS, FAITHFULNESS, GENTLENESS, SELF-CONTROL written on the outside. On the donut bag, this list was formed into the outline of a donut, with a starlike hole with five points. Also, on this bag was a quotation from Ephesians 2:8 — "For it is by grace you have been saved, through faith — and this is not from yourselves, it is the gift of God."

Louis Gencarelli was head of the company. His assistant, Karen Larkin, tells the story: "Louis Gencarelli was an alcoholic for several years. He had come to the end of his rope. In 1989, he was in a hospital getting help, and somehow he called out to God and said, 'Please help me,' and, miraculously, he did help him stop drinking. He went to AA meetings and then he got involved with people who were born-again Christians, who encouraged him to make a commitment to Jesus Christ. When he did that, his life changed dramatically. He was so thankful that the Lord had delivered him from the past that putting the scriptures, which he calls God's word, on his cups and packaging was his way of saying thank you to God. It was not something he meant for everyone to espouse. It was just his way of saying this is how I want to show my

New England's Bess Eaton donut chain had scriptural messages on its donut packaging.

gratefulness to the Lord. We've had letters from people saying, I was down and out and the Lord touched my heart." The Bess Eaton company was started by Louis's father, Angelo, after he learned the donut trade down South. It grew into a large New England chain, and it began to use machines and mixes, still with the original recipe. Karen tells how the name came about: "Louis's grandfather, who was proud of his son, had emigrated from Italy and could just barely speak English. They were testing the donuts one day, and Louis's grandfather said to his son in his broken English, 'This is the bess a' eatin' donut I've ever had.' And so that's how they got the name."

MALASSADA — PORTUGUESE SHROVE TUESDAY DONUT IN HAWAII

Malassadas, the Hawaiian donut-turned-icon, came to Hawaii from Portugal, specifically the island of San Miguel in the Azores, with sugarcane laborers and cowboys at the end of the 19th century.

Lenny Rego says, "My parents are originally from Maui. Their parents came from Portugal to Maui in 1882, then to Honolulu in 1946. They came from the Azores, from Madeira and the other island. It was all contract labor, to work in sugarcane fields."

Lenny's father, Leonard Rego, had always wanted to go into baking. He worked at the Snowflake, a big bakery in Honolulu, from 1946 to 1952. Then he opened up his first shop, a small shop called Leonard's, now Hawaii's most famous malassada bakery.

The malassadas were part of home cooking in Hawaii among the Portuguese, little fried puffs without holes. At that time, Portuguese families ate malassadas especially on Shrove Tuesday, as the last and fattiest treat before Lent, when all such indulgences were forbidden.

DONUTS IN PARADISE
Malassadas have become a Hawaiian icon.

Malassada means badly cooked, and it's disputed whether it has one *s* or two.

Lenny Rego, of Leonard's Bakery, tells it this way: "The idea for the malassada came from my grandmother on my father's side." One day Lenny's grandmother said to her son, "Why don't you make malassadas for Shrove Tuesday?"

"Leonard's was a full-service bakery — cakes, pies, regular," Lenny continues. "He hadn't sold malassadas yet. He thought it was a good idea but the bakers didn't. They thought it was too ethnic. So reluctantly they made it and at first it came out heavy and oily. They worked on it to make it more light and palatable. The shop opened on July 1, '52, and he started selling malassadas on Shrove Tuesday of 1953. They became popular."

Thus the malassadas were introduced into Hawaii's commercial life by a grandmother who trotted out her old recipe. This was the first time they were made and sold commercially. The fried treats were an overnight success, serving as the bakery's trademark and subsequently one of Hawaii's most visible foods. They jumped out of Portuguese homes into the bakery, where they became available to all Hawaiians, who bought them and loved them and then elevated them into a Hawaiian icon.

Lenny says: "My grandma passed away when I was about twelve, but she saw the success of the malassada."

Leonard Jr.'s bakery has "malasadas" and "Malasada Babies."

I say, "Your grandmother introduced the malassada to Hawaii!"

"As far I know that could well be. Word has gotten around that you can't leave Hawaii until you go to Leonard's and have a malassada. It has become associated with Hawaii now. We've been fortunate. It's been around for fifty-one years," he says.

Leonard's Bakery, where the original malassada was introduced, now has Malassada Beanie Babies. There is now also Leonard Junior's, opened by Lenny Rego, who as a child was his father's first little taste-tester. It also has Malassada Mobiles selling Malassada Puffs.

In Hawaii there are the malassada traditionalists, those who maintain that the taste of the original item is not only enough but also the way it should be. One said, "Our biggest compliment is when people say 'This is the way my *vovo* [grandmother]

Apple Cider Donuts

Served with hot or cold cider, these donuts — glazed, dusted with cinnamon sugar, or left plain — are the stuff of autumn memories. *Makes 20 donuts*

2½ cups all-purpose flour

1½ teaspoons baking powder

1 teaspoon baking soda

½ teaspoon ground cinnamon

½ cup granulated sugar

3 tablespoons unsalted butter, softened

1 egg

¼ cup apple cider or juice

¼ cup milk

1 tablespoon vanilla extract

1 medium apple (McIntosh, Jonagold, or Golden Delicious)

Vegetable oil for deep frying

1 cup confectioners' sugar, optional

1 tablespoon ground cinnamon, optional

2 tablespoons apple juice, optional

1. In a large bowl, combine the flour, baking powder, soda, and cinnamon. Make a well in the center.

2. In a small bowl, cream together the sugar and butter. Beat in the egg.

3. Add the apple cider, milk, and vanilla. Beat all together. Pour into the center of the dry ingredients and stir until smooth.

4. Peel, core, and finely chop the apple and stir into the batter.

5. Cover and chill the dough for 1 hour.

6. Place half of the dough on a floured surface, knead lightly, and roll out to approximately ⅜ inch thick. Cut with a floured 2½-inch donut cutter.

7. In a wok or skillet, heat the oil to 375°F on a deep-fat thermometer. Fry the dough for 1 to 2 minutes on each side, until golden brown. Do not overcrowd. Drain on absorbent paper and dust or glaze while warm.

8. To dust the donuts, sift the confectioners' sugar with the ground cinnamon; sprinkle over the donuts. To make a glaze, stir the apple juice into the sugar and cinnamon mixture; brush over the donuts.

made them.'" And there are the iconoclasts and innovators, those who are filling them with passion fruit or pepper jelly or cappuccino cream or ice cream. The ice-cream idea happened when an ice-cream cone fell into a batch of malassada dough and became "Hawaii's Own Fried Malassada Ice Cream," sold in a store with the same name.

Lenny says, "The malassada connoisseurs want the original; they don't want it to be corrupted. Others put filling in, so we decided to do that, and I registered the mark — Malassada Puffs. Once, only Leonard's made malassadas, but now a lot of people make them. Hawaii loves malassadas and some are religious in terms of the brand. They won't eat anybody else's. Our busiest malassada day is Shrove Tuesday. We probably sell 32,000–40,000 that day between the two companies."

THE ORCHARDS OF CONCKLIN

It is a clear early November evening in Rockland County, New York. The Orchards of Concklin are on South Mountain Road, and while this is not an alp, it is on a high bluff above a wide expanse of the Hudson River, the mighty Hudson, with hills and cliffs rising from it. The orchards, here since the 1700s, are in a very rural corner of the world, with farms and fields rolling down the hill, and not much else around except apple trees and a stone hut. Concklin has a shop with apples and donuts and sundries for sale. There are large buckets of apples of every kind, all grown here. In the fall there is an inflatable haunted house and an inflatable tractor. The apple cider donuts are well known here and in New York City, where they are sold at the farmers' market.

The donuts are in little see-through plastic bags with the inviting logo of the orchard, a farmhouse set in a copse, printed in blue. They are apple cider, plain and with powdered sugar, and they are just the thing to warm you up at dusk on a cold night. Over the

fields a full clear moon is rising in the dark blue sky. Later there will be a completely visible eclipse of the full moon, a rare sky show.

Linda Concklin Hill is arranging some goods on the shelves. She has straight blond hair and smooth white skin (with apple cheeks), and she is wearing jeans and a sweatshirt. She is straightforward, smart and plain talking. Her family has owned the orchard since the 1700s. She is who she is, she runs a great farm and shop, and she is trying to preserve this way of life. The donuts are a part of it.

Out the back door is the old wooden barn, with rafters and rickety stairs leading to an attic. Bins of apples are all over, up and down. It smells of apple. There are tools and sacks of farm stuff everywhere. And outside is a stone hut surrounded by apple trees and fields stretching in every direction and nothing else, no built stuff, just the huge yellow moon and the darkening sky. It's a corner that New Yorkers don't get to see much, even though it's only 45 minutes from the city, a world of farm and apple and life lived from what the earth produces and what you can make of it.

Linda Concklin Hill says, "My maiden name is Concklin. I grew up on the farm, went away, and got married. When I got divorced I came home again. Back in the sixties, before pick-your-own and before greenmarkets, that's when we started making donuts. We were looking for new ways to

entice people into our retail farm store. We sold mostly apples and a few other things." Linda says, "We are apple- and farm-oriented,

so everything we made had to have apple in it. What we were interested in was whatever we had to do to sell apples. We chopped 'em and put 'em in cookies and ground 'em and put 'em in cider. We put the cider in the donuts."

I'm looking for the apple cider donuts at the farmers' market in Union Square, New York City. The Concklin stand is just there, without fanfare, and the man behind it is black and has dread locks. He's selling the apple cider donuts. They are near beautiful colored eggs with rich eggy flavor, from Araucana hens. And arugula flowers and buckwheat leaves. And nasturtium blossoms in yellow and orange. The Jamaican man brings the donuts from the orchard to sell to black-clad, gold-bangled dames with high heels and bags of microgreens for cocktail parties.

"Calvin works in the bakery and he's been doing greenmarkets and he's learning to talk to people and he's doing really well," Linda says.

She says that "part of the joy of farming here is that we have an amalgamation of people we've been able to hang out with. We get along well with other people, you respect

Linda Concklin Hill, of the Orchards of Concklin. Their apple cider donuts are famous in the Hudson Valley and in New York City.

Roasted Granny Smith Apple Beignets

Gerry Hayden, the chef of New York's Amuse Restaurant, says, "I really didn't consider it a donut, but it is a donut. I wanted to have a nice roasted apple inside and crunchy texture outside. The cider reduction and the maple syrup ice cream just followed naturally." *Makes 4 servings*

GRANNY SMITH APPLE RINGS

  ½ cup sugar
  ¼ vanilla bean
  1 Granny Smith apple, peeled but not cored

1. Preheat oven to 350°F.

2. Mix sugar and vanilla.

3. Slice the apple into four pieces ½ inch thick. Don't put in water. Core the centers and toss in vanilla and sugar.

4. Bake for 3 minutes on a silicon baking mat. Flip the apple rings over. Bake for 3 more minutes — the apples should be lightly soft and have no green color. Remove from oven and let cool.

FRITTER BATTER

  ¾ cup milk
  3 tablespoons browned butter
  1 teaspoon vanilla extract
  1 egg yolk
  1 cup all-purpose flour
  2 tablespoons sugar
  1 teaspoon baking powder
  ½ teaspoon nutmeg
  ½ teaspoon salt
  ½ teaspoon lemon zest
  2 egg whites

1. Warm the milk and butter to the touch. Stir in the vanilla and yolk.

2. In a bowl, combine the flour, 1 tablespoon of the sugar, and baking powder, nutmeg, salt, and the lemon zest.

3. Pour the milk mixture over the dry ingredients and combine.

4. In a separate bowl, whip the egg whites and remaining sugar to a stiff peak and fold into mixture. Cover until ready to use.

APPLE REDUCTION SAUCE

  ½ cup plus 2 tablespoons sugar
  ¼ vanilla bean, scraped
  ½ cup apple juice
  1 cinnamon stick

1. Combine everything in a pot and bring to 228°F.

2. Strain and put in an ice bath until cool.

APPLE CHIPS

½ cup sugar

1 cup water

¼ cup lemon juice

1 Granny Smith apple

1. Preheat oven to 210°F.

2. Bring the sugar, water, and lemon juice to a boil in a saucepan. Cut the apple into ⅛-inch-thick slices.

3. Spread out the slices in a casserole dish or heat-resistant bowl and pour the hot lemon liquid over top. Let the liquid cool to the touch, then transfer the apples to a baking tray lined with a silicon baking sheet, shaking off excess liquid.

4. Bake for about 1 hour, or until dry and crispy. Remove from oven and flatten, gently.

MAPLE SUGAR ICE CREAM

2 cups cream

2 cups milk

¾ cup maple sugar

8 egg yolks

⅓ cup toasted walnuts, roughly chopped

1. In a saucepan, bring the cream and milk to a boil. Remove from heat and whisk in the maple sugar until dissolved.

2. Temper the egg yolks by mixing a small amount of the hot liquid into the yolks and then whisking that mixture into the hot mixture in the saucepan.

3. Pour into a clean pot and, stirring constantly, cook to 185°F (84°C). Strain through two layers of cheesecloth and cool in an ice bath, stirring occasionally.

4. Freeze mixture in an ice-cream maker. Put in the freezer to set slightly. Fold in the nuts and harden in freezer.

ASSEMBLY

1. Heat a pot of oil to 320°F and keep at that temperature.

2. Toss the apple rings in the fritter batter until nicely coated, then remove from batter with a finger in the center of the apple to prevent the batter from cooking over the hole.

3. Cook until brown on both sides, remove, and place on paper towels.

4. Drizzle a plate with Apple Reduction Sauce and place a scoop of Maple Sugar Ice Cream with an Apple Chip on top on the plate. Place an apple ring against the ice cream and serve.

everybody, everybody's allowed to be a little different, it's part of the fun. In the seventies we were the first to employ a Vietnamese. It was very difficult because we said, 'Okay, what have you done?' And the Vietnamese man said, 'Well, I know to shoot a gun.' And it's like — okay. But that was his life experience. He was twenty-two years old and that's all he'd done all his life, having come from Vietnam. We have Mexicans, Dominicans, Ecuadorans, Americans, of course."

Mrs. Glickman, who works at the orchard, tells me she is Jewish, from South America, an Argentinian Jew, "but I am blond and blue-eyed. I am from Poland and Russia, I speak Hebrew and Italian and Castilian and French and other languages. Here you have Spanish and Dominicans, and we are surrounded by the Hasidic community."

Of her own history, she says, "I made *aliyah* to Israel and I met my husband — Yankee, go home and please take me with you, so he did. He's American. New York is too big for me and we came up here."

She says that this is a very old farm, one of the few left from the 1700s. The orchard has been owned by the Concklin family since then.

Linda Concklin tells me, "The family came to Salem, Massachusetts, in 1637. We say we got chased out when they were chasing the witches, but the truth is that that part of the family was Irish. They came over in the glass industry, and that went kaput. In 1712, they bought our property. My mom was a Palatine German, so they had moved into the Hudson Valley to do pine tar to seal the ships. That industry was also broken, and those people were just deserted there."

Linda says, "We do have a scratch recipe for donuts but the one that most people like is a combination of mixes with stuff we add to it, so it's like a personalized thing. The original mix we were using they stopped making; we liked that mix but we can't get it. The original mix was a DCA Golden Dipt mix."

FROM THE ORCHARDS OF CONCKLIN WEB SITE

The Concklins first came to America in 1637 from Nottingham, England. John and Anias Conklyn were members of the first Presbyterian Church of Salem, Massachusetts. Nicholas Concklin traveled up the Hudson to Haverstraw, New York and walked inland to the Pomona region. There he bought 400 acres of the Kakiat patent Lot No. 1, in 1711, settling in the region in 1718. George Washington was supposed to have slept here as a guest of Lieutenant Nicholas Concklin. J. Raymond Concklin, who was born in 1912, operated the farm with his wife, Ardell E. Concklin, who died in 1990 at the age of 72. In that time period he operated the farm together with his son, Richard, and daughter, Linda. When he died, in 1993, they took over the farm and are still running it.

I tell her, "That's my family's mix!"

Linda: "We do about 40,000 bags of donuts per year, six to a bag. Add on all the ones I eat.

"We couldn't understand why our dogs were getting so fat. One of the bakers was popping the dogs donuts, so of course the dog sat right outside the door. They all gained fifty pounds, we had to put a stop to it."

THEY'RE MCDONUTS

People are mesmerized by the machine. It's a rave. It's the same machine that has been in use for 100 years, almost. Things have come full circle. The Rube Goldberg contraption, Homer Price's diamond-ring-in-donuts machine, is in the window of McDonald's. McDonald's in New York City was not attracting enough business after 9/11, so it did what my grandfather did: put a donut machine in the window, and that is solving the problem.

Julio, a manager, says, "Your grandfather was a genius. Sweetheart, I have in my head an idea for a fries machine too."

He says the donut machine brings business into McDonald's.

"Are the donut shops mad at you?" I ask.

"Hey, what can you do?" he says. "It's McDonuts. Sweetheart, have some."

The machine is in a locked glass compartment in the front of the shop right by the window. You can't get in. It's the same old Wonderful Almost Human Automatic Donut

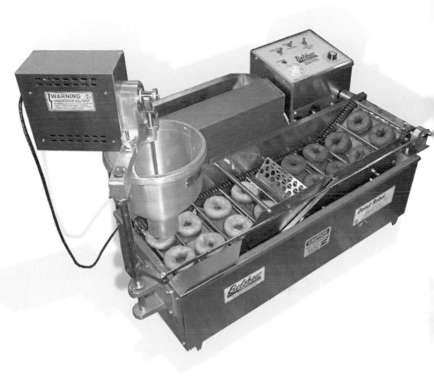

Machine, that wonder of wonders — dough in, mix, cut, plop, fry, dry, drop into the plastic basket that rotates to cool. People outside are gaping at it. Maybe they've never seen one before.

Irwin Kruger, New York franchise owner, says, "We feel the machine is one of the great inventions. People love watching the donuts plop down and then flip over and then come out beautifully symmetrical, and it's visually great." This was also in line with the notions of the founder of McDonald's, Ray Kroc, and "his original architecture, where customers could look inside the freestanding McDonald's restaurants and see the food being prepared. It was exactly the kind of operation that made McDonald's," Kruger says.

The neon sign in the window flashes on and off. McDonuts, red letters except for the yellow *O* in a donut shape. Mini McDonuts are 12 for $1.89, a bargain. Today's flavor is apple crisp. The donuts look nice. They are neat little rings, about the size of half a normal donut. They taste gummy and doughy and what papier-mâché would taste like if you ate it. Sort of like a vaguely sweet hamburger roll. But that doesn't seem to matter. People buy them and love them. They eat the whole box at once.

Irwin Kruger says, "It's hard to hate a donut. It's easy to love it, for all the reasons. Donuts are very friendly. So it's fun for us to have the opportunity to sell them at McDonald's, where people are surprised. March 2002 we did 34th and 8th, and then September 42nd

MCDONUTS
McDonald's in Times Square lures customers with a donut machine in the window, just as did Donut King Adolph Levitt.

Street. We made a batch of funnel cakes at home, in the kitchen. The idea of fried dough led me to think about the donuts."

The McDonuts dozen comes in a small white box like a hamburger box, white plasticized cardboard with cheery red graphics on a white ground. The logo on the box is Danny Donut, alias McDonald's longtime Speedee. Danny Donut/Speedee struts on the box in red, chest out, proud donut face smiling, carrying the flag for donuts, toque on head. He's running and he's carrying a sign that says, I'M SPEEDEE. Wink, toque, strut, donut face as smile. He wears red-and-white-striped pants and a red bow tie. He's happy. He jumps up to the top of a McDonald's arch that appears on the box.

Irwin Kruger says, "The Speedee was the original McDonald's logo that they had in the mid-fifties, when they started the company. It's a throwback to the original concept of mass feeding and merchandising. We put six donuts in there quickly, and they don't get squashed. They seem like they are nice and comfortable. These particular small ones are perfect for grab and go."

Irwin Kruger was born and raised a New Yorker, and he got involved with McDonald's 35 years ago, in 1973, in Rhode Island and New Jersey. "I sold my stores in other areas, and I own and operate seven stores in Manhattan, out of 13,000 in the US, 690 in the New York tri-state area, 75 in Manhattan.

"Where we are there are thirty-eight movie screens. We are adjacent to the New Amsterdam Theater, where the *Lion King* is. 42nd Street is a brand unto itself. People have heard of that street."

He says that he saw the famous Belshaw machine at Dreesen's in East Hampton: "I was very impressed with the engineering of this piece of equipment we had that your grandfather designed, and in its reliability. The Belshaw reputation was great. They couldn't have been nicer."

Then Kruger got McDonald's interested in it: "The CEO was here — I brought him to the West 42nd Store, which was under construction. I surprised him, and he loved the way we had set up, and the location." Kruger got the go-ahead.

"There's no real identification of McDonald's with donuts yet. They generate a lot of goodwill. It's fun to see the theater effect of having them right in the window." There's also a twist to the names. A daily standby is "Majestic Vanilla," lifting that flavor from "plain vanilla" to majesty. There's "Orange Dream," with real orange juice. Kruger says, "When you mix that with powdered sugar, it tastes like a creamsicle. These are all fantasy, dreamy flavors." The donuts are a success.

Kruger wanted to give something back to his beloved city, something "quirky and New York." McDonuts, a contribution to New York pop culture, "fit that bill."

PROFESSOR OF DONUTS

I came across Kevin Murphy's article in *Food History News*, a newsletter published in Islesboro, Maine. "Doughnuts, which have gone from homemade goodie to roadside novelty in the century and a half since their modern incarnation, were an essential part of the familial rituals of our Maine summer vacations starting in the 1960s."

Kevin is gathering stories of small donut producers and memories from donut eaters. It's not every day you find an art history professor researching donuts.

Kevin says he did a consulting project on motels as examples of roadside architecture. Motels started as mom-and-pop shops and "got swallowed up by chains."

Kevin writes, "During the 1950s, the 40-billion-dollar federal interstate highway system was begun, and enthusiasm for automobile travel reached its zenith. Doughnut shops — along with motels, drive-in restaurants, and other enterprises — became part of a new landscape geared to the automobile. One strategy used by roadside entrepreneurs to make their establishments visible to speeding motorists was to super-size images of their products. From coast to coast, carry-out restaurants sprouted colossal doughnuts from their roofs."

Later, "Charged with positive associations with small-scale home production, the doughnut — like other foods and commodities — was more and more the result of mechanized, factory-based production."

FROM IMMIGRANT TO PRESIDENT

Coffee An', Westport, Connecticut

The water on the Connecticut shore is full of sailboats, in bright sunshine, no clouds. In a little cluster of shops on the way to the main street is Coffee An', as the locals call it, right next to the hardware store. This afternoon around two it is empty, except for a few old-timers sitting on the padded black counter stools. There are some tables with chairs that have tape on the seats, and there's a blackboard with chalk writing telling about the kinds of donuts and other stuff. Some plastic Greek urns with gods and goddesses are part of the décor. And in the cases are the best donut-shop donuts you could possibly eat.

George Vlandis, employee and father of the owner, Elias Vlandis, says, "We are here four o'clock, and we make the donuts. We added few extras like coconut and cinnamon buns, and they moving really good. We have customers from New York, Greenwich, we have a lot of writers over here, and a lot of times we have customers from Boston, California, Texas." When you eat them, you remember why donuts got so popular. The glazed converted a cake donut lover, and the old-fashioned converted me, a glazed fan.

The Vlandises are proudly Greek and proudly American too. They started in pizza and moved to donuts. Elias, in his late 30s, has bright blue eyes and black hair and a winning smile. He looks authentically Greek, with the face of a hero in a war scene off one of those famous Greek vases. He lifts up the tray of cinnamon and chocolate donuts so we can see better. Then when we are not looking, he packs boxes of donuts for us to take back home on the train. The doormen in my building polish them off in about three minutes.

George Vlandis, Elias's father, answers the phone, "Hello Coffee An' . . ."

He has a lot to say, and he says it in an identifiably Greek accent combined with his own idiosyncratic intonation.

"I came from Athens, okay? My father used to be a baker over there. Nineteen seventy I open up the Pizza Palace in Fairfield."

I ask how he came. "I came to this country by boat. Why I came? For better living. I have relatives, they invite me over, they offer me jobs, place to live. And that's it. After, I was working with my uncle for a while. In supermarket and luncheonette."

I ask, "That was your first job?"

"Yes. And after that I left, my uncle and I opened up the pizza place in Fairfield. I was the first one over there, good place, good business. Okay? So I was over there for sixteen years. In 1989 I left over there, I sold the place, I thought I was gonna retire. My son was graduated from college, after that I discover he didn't want to work in the office. So we decided we change from the pizza to the donut shop. This place was for sale over here, this place been here for forty-five years. Coffee An'. Then I bought the shop. I took over 1991."

You could easily miss this donut mecca in its unassuming little enclave of shops stuck on a road going from the train to the town. But people know it's there and it's packed in the mornings. That's why they close every day at three. It's a nice little shop, the kind of local soda shop that used to be and isn't anymore, like the donuts it makes, totally from scratch, no mix, no machine.

"It was already making donuts. The only thing — it wasn't doing that kind of business. We was making the donuts more tasty, and we did a lot of extra more business than what the guys was doing before. They was making homemade donuts already, but after we took over we was making much better, better-quality ingredients.

"I'm here myself now eleven years. So then three, four years ago I turn it to my son. So instead of me being retired, I work for my son." This relationship clearly is working.

On the wall there are pictures and more pictures. Then you look at them and you see that they are of presidents and other politicians, Bill and Hillary Clinton and George

PRESIDENTIAL FAN
Bill Clinton is a famous donut eater. Coffee An' sent him donuts at the White House. After that, he told his Cabinet that Coffee An' had the best.

Bush and Al Gore, and that the Greek people who own and run this shop are with them at dinners and rallies, and that there are notes thanking them for the amazing donuts.

These donuts have been to the White House and around the block. "One time I sent donuts to the White House," George says. "Through a friend of ours who was a doctor, his daughter was working at the White House right next to the president's office. One day she said, 'Okay, George, I'm going to the White House now, how about send me some donuts for President Clinton?' Okay? So I says, Okay, so I put few donuts in a box. I thought she was joke around, you know? She took 'em, okay? And a few days after I receive a picture of President Clinton, you know? 'Good luck, and God bless you, and thanks for the donuts.'

"After that, I was invited to Stamford, in Marriott Hotel, they have dinner. Then he came to Westport, I was invited, then I met Vice President Gore. So you know . . ."

Some of the pictures are in the National Hall in Westport, for a political fund-raiser. "With my wife, and I took my son over there too, and Vice President Gore promised my son, he says, 'If I ever become presi-dent, Elias, I'm gonna come to your store too, you know, for donuts.' Gore goes, he says, 'George,' he says to all the people, you know, over there in the dinner, 'every morning if we have breakfast with the Cabinet, the presi-dent he says to his Cabinet, have you ever been in Westport? The best donuts are in Westport, the little place, call 'em Coffee An'."

Celebrities come here just to buy the donuts: "Then we have Paul Newman was coming over here, a lot of famous people they are coming here, you know," George says. "I went with the president at his hotel in Stamford, and I was talking with Clinton, and right behind me was Mr. Newman, and he goes, 'You look familiar,' and I said, 'I'm the one who makes your pastrami sandwiches, the tuna melt,' and he says, 'Oh, you're George from Coffee An'."

I tell George that I saw a picture of him and his wife in the newspaper with a bishop of the Greek Church. "We were on TV and in the news. People tell us we make the best donuts, they try everything, they say no com-parison. We got a good name."

He says to me with an air of finality, "You got enough stories, that's it. Okay? We are doing really good."

I ask if he would be willing to give me any of his recipes.

"This, no." He laughs. "Sally, I'm sorry. Lotta people, they ask us about that. We try to keep secret. You want donuts, I send 'em to you."

SOME EXTREMES —
DINER DONUTS, SORT OF

Everything about the Lunchbox Food Company is unexpected. First, it's not really lunchbox food. The chefs have been at some of the top temples of gastronomy. Shawn, the dessert chef, made donuts filled with plum compote at Daniel restaurant. He grew up in the Bronx, and he trained to be an electrician. But he would come home every day after school and he'd be "cooking, cooking, cooking," he says. He still lives in the Bronx.

The Lunchbox is really a diner, with a counter and swivel stools and booths. Its sign is neon and it's on a stretch of the West Side Highway that is full of car shops and not much else. But it's a diner reinvented. The crowd is more Soho art than car mechanic. On a warm summer afternoon, it's dining al fresco, with salads made with the likes of frisée and goat Gouda. But also there are "Doughnuts — assortment varies seasonally, one dollar plain, a dollar fifty filled." The donuts are all homemade. At lunch and breakfast they come as they are, and at dinner they are called churros, to dip in hot or cold chocolate.

Shawn is 29. His uncle, a chef at Pork University, was his model. He has cooked at restaurants around New York — the Judson Grill, a fine restaurant in midtown, and Daniel, New York's fanciest, but "it was too busy for me," he says.

Donuts? He's made them just about every way, from the "plum puffs" to his favorite, coconut.

In 1993 there was the nation's first diner conference, under the auspices of "a group of roadside archivists called the Society for Commercial Archeology," according to the *New York Times*. Dr. John Levine, professor of psychiatry, gave a talk about the "psychological appeal of the diner," saying that diners induce "a pleasant melancholia, a dreamlike state, evocative of memory and loss," like the memories of childhood brought on by Proust's eating of the madeleine, and that "[t]he diner today provides the setting for the same trick, except with donuts and coffee."

Picarones

The food of Peru reflects native abundance and combines various cultural inheritances — African, Spanish, Incan. Picarones are the number one typical dessert in Peru, both a fast-food item and a homemade tradition in grandmother's kitchen. Calle Ocho combines several Latin culinary traditions in a Nuevo Latino New York restaurant. *Makes about 20 picarones*

1 pound sweet potatoes
4 tablespoons dry yeast
2 tablespoons sugar
¾ cup warm milk
2 pounds plus 2 ounces all-purpose
   flour
1¼ cup sugar
5 eggs
3 tablespoons salt
2 tablespoons vanilla extract
1 tablespoon cinnamon
6 ounces butter
   Vegetable oil for frying
   Caster sugar for sprinkling

1. Preheat oven to 325°F.

2. Wrap the sweet potatoes individually in aluminum foil and bake for 25 minutes, or until soft. Unwrap, remove the skin, and let cool.

3. In the bowl of an electric mixer, dissolve the yeast and sugar in the warm milk and let stand for about 3 minutes. Combine the sweet potatoes with the milk mixture and add the next six ingredients except the butter and mix for 1 hour. Then add the butter and mix for 10 more minutes, or until the dough becomes elastic.

4. Remove the dough from the mixing bowl, place it in a floured bowl, and let rise for 25 to 30 minutes. When risen, knead the dough and let rise again, then repeat this process twice more. Roll out the dough on a floured surface and cut it into donut shapes.

5. Heat the oil to 375°F and fry the donuts until golden. Drain on paper towels, then sprinkle with caster sugar.

SILK ROAD MOCHA, NEW YORK CITY

There is a cyber café in Chinatown called Silk Road Mocha. Hillary Clinton went there to revive Chinatown after the SARS scare. It has espresso and tapioca drinks — a Chinese favorite — and Krispy Kreme donuts. The espresso menu has hazelnut silkaccino and caramel macchiato. The Chinese menu has "bubble drinks," Chinese drinks — green milk tea, or kumquat fruit tea, or lychee juice, or taro milk shake, or red bean smoothie. Silk Road Mocha has Chinese teas and Barbara Bush on TV. It has a banner with Silk Road Mocha on it and another with Krispy Kreme donuts on it. It's a café and teahouse combined, with an injection of cyber equipment and donuts, for cutting-edge status.

Outside is Chinatown honky-tonk — red-tasseled lamps, overstuffed trinket stalls,

The *New York Times* says of Silk Road Mocha: "The shape of Chinatown to come? An art gallery and cybercafe, with pork buns and lattes."

windup toys, restaurants with colored paper lanterns, and shops with teas and candied ginger and herbs and dried fish. At the front of Silk Road Mocha are several computer stations, and inside are photos featuring American flags as backdrop to the Chinese drinks and espressos. Inside the front cases are Krispy Kreme donuts in glazed, chocolate, and cinnamon, and they are mostly gone.

Silk Road Mocha is a cyber cafe in Chinatown with Chinese teas, espresso, and Krispy Kreme donuts.

Boston Crème Donuts

This recipe for chocolate-glazed, custard-filled donuts appeared in Jane and Michael Stern's *Blue Plate Specials and Blue Ribbon Chefs*. They discovered the donut at Mike's Donuts in Everett, Massachusetts. *Makes 18 donuts*

DONUTS

- 1 cup milk
- 4 tablespoons butter, plus more for greasing
- ½ cup plus ½ teaspoon sugar
- ½ teaspoon salt
- 1 egg
- 1 package yeast
- ¼ cup warm water (105 to 115°F)
- 3 cups all-purpose flour, plus ½ cup
- ½ teaspoon vanilla
- Oil for deep frying

FILLING

- 1 cup refrigerated prepared vanilla pudding

GLAZE

- 2 ounces semisweet chocolate
- ½ ounce unsweetened chocolate
- 1 tablespoon butter
- 1 cup confectioners' sugar
- ½ teaspoon vanilla
- 2 to 3 tablespoons hot water

1. To make the donuts, scald the milk with 4 tablespoons butter, ½ cup of the sugar, and salt, stirring to dissolve the sugar. Cool to lukewarm, then beat in the egg. Proof the yeast in the water with ½ teaspoon sugar until foamy.

2. In a large mixing bowl, combine 3 cups of the flour, the milk mixture, vanilla, and yeast mixture. Beat until smooth. Add more flour, if needed, to make a soft dough that pulls from the sides of the bowl.

3. Turn the dough onto a floured board and knead 5 minutes, until smooth. Place in a greased bowl, cover lightly, and let rise in a warm place, until double in bulk.

4. Punch down dough and place on lightly floured surface. Roll to ½-inch thickness. Cut with 2½-inch biscuit cutter. Place cut pieces 2 inches apart on a floured baking sheet, cover lightly, and let rise 45 minutes, or until nearly doubled.

5. Heat the oil in a deep fryer or heavy pan to 365°F. Fry the donuts, a few at a time, 3 minutes on the first side, or until golden. Turn with a slotted spoon and fry 2 to 3 more minutes. Remove and drain on paper towels. Cool.

6. Make a small slit in the side of each donut. Fill a pastry bag with the filling. Use a plain tip to push about 2 teaspoons of the filling inside each donut.

7. Make the glaze by melting both chocolates with the butter in a small, heavy saucepan. Stir in the confectioners' sugar and vanilla until smooth. Beat in enough water for easy-spreading consistency. Spread atop each filled donut. Serve immediately or within a few hours. Any leftovers must be refrigerated because of the pudding filling.

ITALIAN DONUTS

Siena is one of the oldest cities in Italy. It rises from a crazy-quilt landscape of hills patched with olive groves and vineyards and stone farms and castles, the landscape that is the backdrop for many Italian paintings. Its streets are still medieval. The buildings are in a brown color that all American school kids know from their crayon boxes as Burnt Siena. The center of the city is the piazza with its medieval palace and high tower, where the famous Palio horse race, with its ritual of banners tossed and swung and swirled in a kind of dance or joust, takes place. In this city out of time are narrow alleys with modern shops in the old buildings, like Nannini, a café with donuts! This is as far from modern city streets as you can get, but there are the donuts, called *bombolini* or *zeppole.*

Seven

AMAZING DONUTS

There are good donuts, bad donuts, and occasionally original or amazing donuts. They are being created by chefs and donut shops, and they are made by hand or by machine. Behind the donuts are the New Masters of donuts, a bit like the Old Masters of art.

Krispy Kreme rules the street, with frequently overheard streetside rhapsodies about its donuts. Mark Isreal is unchallenged as World's Only Rose Petal Doughnut Creator. Rudy DeSanti is consummate Donut Raconteur, with stories from Roman hills to the butcher shop that turned into a famous donut shop too, with donut machine in the window, in celebrity-studded East Hampton, New York.

Each has a donut discovery. It might be an old donut rediscovered, like the favorite Chock Full O'Nuts Whole Wheat Donut. It might be new, like Marcus Samuelsson's Green Tea Donut. It might be, well, borrowed, like Chef Mavro's Passion Fruit Malassada, an elegant riff on Hawaii's popular snack. It might even be blue, like Isreal's Yankee donut with blueberry stripes.

I t was simple. No icing, no organic ingredients, no fancy frills, no poetic names invoking tropical fruits or the mists of autumn. It had no pretensions. It was just a donut, but without the cold-fat texture and taste, and with a delectable fresh nuttiness that made you want another and another. It was irresistible. It did not dazzle with sequins but conquered with sincerity, and with the only quality that matters, taste. It was itself, no airs, no affectations. Once you tasted it, you were spoiled, in some cases forever, for other donuts. For those who were lucky enough to have it, the Chock Full O'Nuts Whole Wheat Donut, from the '60s and '70s, was everybody's favorite. It was a wondrously crunchy, grainy orb with a toasted taste that somehow chased away the fried fattiness of donuts. Few people cared then about health food. It did not cry out at you, "I am whole wheat and healthy." It was just plain delicious.

The New York operations manager of Chock Full O'Nuts, Tony Bonavia, says, "Recently, there is a lot of emphasis on the Whole Wheat Donut that Chock Full O'Nuts was famous for. Every time I open a new location, I hear, 'Do you have the Whole Wheat Donut?' There's much more buzz about donuts in recent years."

Many people have said to me, "Do you remember the Chock Full O'Nuts Whole Wheat Donut? That was the best one."

Everyone loved it, hicks and city slickers. Everyone who ate it then and remembers mentions it now in hushed, reverent tones within moments of starting to talk about donuts. You have to be of a certain age to remember it, since it died out decades ago, when Chock went coffee and forsook its food items.

What made it so good? People at Chock say that the whole wheat content made it different, that it was fried longer, and that it turned out crunchier and crispier than your average donut. People have tried to copy it — the Cupcake Café in New York City has an orange whole wheat donut invented in memory of its taste. But no one has duplicated it yet.

The fact that such a delicious item has disappeared makes it even more legendary, even more sacrosanct, surrounded with an aura of mystery and venerability and myth and desire. Where has this donut gone? Who dared to get rid of it? It is spoken of longingly, with a faraway look, rendering it sacred, untouchable. Unparalleled love, donut nostalgia, and the new explosion of donuts into the public consciousness have made the Chock Full O'Nuts donut into the Holy Grail.

Today Krispy Kreme is capitalizing on youth and its short memory. Now rhapsodies are for Krispy Kreme Hot Doughnuts. The Holy Grail has been shoved aside for this new donut icon, the Krispy Kreme. Or Krispy Kreme is the New Holy Grail.

But wait. By some miracle, or because of the mounting chorus of voices of those who still remember, Chock, as it is now called, is bringing this donut, the Holy Grail, back to life. The Whole Wheat Donut is returning, with a maximum of hype, flair, and secrecy. Since Sara Lee bought Chock, newfound funds are going into reviving it. Bonavia says,

"I really want to make it a big surprise, so people come back and say that it is just like I remembered. We always knew there was a buzz about the Whole Wheat Donut. I think we should make a big splash."

A second coming. A donut resurrection.

MARK ISREAL, OF NEW YORK'S DOUGHNUT PLANT

Mark Isreal is an unexpected Doughnut Man. His is a small shop, independent, and it is New York's most famous donut shop at the moment, the Doughnut Plant. Outside the shop are bialys and Chinese food, and there are Lower East Side artists and bums, and there are Hasidim striding down the street in round black hats and sidelocks.

Mark is tall, and he's a sweet guy with an earring, a Jew from the South who came to New York with nothing in his pockets. His grandfather was a Finnish Jew, a baker, who made delicious donuts that stuck in his grandson's mind.

Mark Isreal started by delivering donuts on his bike. Now his Doughnut Plant is New York City's most famous donut shop.

"I grew up in North Carolina, in Greensboro," Mark says. "I had always heard about my grandfather's bakery. There weren't very many bakeries in Greensboro, so I always heard how good my grandfather's pastries, donuts, cookies, bread, everything was. They did it from scratch. It was called the College Pastry Shop. He made up the donut recipe in the thirties."

Today Mark is wearing a red bandanna, perhaps in honor of his grandfather's cowboy days. When he talks about his family it is with real fondness. "My grandfather died when I was three. Herman, he came here from Finland, he was a Finnish Jew. He was a cowboy in the U.S. and then he opened a bakery. I have this great picture of him. Can I show it to you? He looks so immigrant.

"There's his first bakery, and look, there's the donut. There's our donut, see this? He learned to bake in the Army in World War I, but then we found this picture of him when he was a teenager in a bakery, so he was a baker before he went to the war. He worked in St. Paul, Minnesota, in a baking equipment company, and then he was a cowboy in Ripley, Tennessee."

Mark says, in his expressive way, "He was a cowboy! He used to herd animals and he sold horses. I asked my dad, 'He killed animals?' and I was like, 'Tell me he didn't do that!' I'm vegetarian. He was like, 'He herded wild horses.' "

Mark says, "My grandfather had all these recipes in a box in the attic. I saw the donut recipe. Dad and I made the donuts, and they were so good it just stuck in my mind." After he came to New York, Mark got tired of being poor and decided to make his grandfather's donuts in the kitchen of his Lower East Side apartment, changing their composition to contain all organic ingredients. He spread flour and fat everywhere, took the donuts, put them on his bike, rode all over town to coffee shops, and all the donuts sold. He used blueberries and rose petals and cashew nuts. People loved them. He went for the top, Balducci's and Zabar's, and began to be called the Doughnut Man, since people couldn't remember his name but knew him for his donuts. Hey, Doughnut Man, what do you have today?

"I'd be on my bicycle delivering the donuts and people would yell at me, 'Hey Doughnut Man!' I was on TV and in papers because of the bike."

He got known at the greenmarket, where he bought organic milk and raspberries for glazes. Now, nine years later, the Doughnut Plant is famous for organic donuts.

"I moved to New York when I was seventeen. I was a busboy and a waiter. I'm forty now. Then I was working in a wholesale bakery. One day I went to a coffee shop on Avenue A, a dive coffee shop called Limbo. I said, 'If I made something, would you buy it?'

[the manager] said, 'What are you gonna bring?' I said, 'I could bring donuts.' The day I went to the coffee shop — I don't even know if I knew what I was gonna make. I thought I would make a couple dozen donuts in my apartment and sell them to this one coffee shop. And he ate them and he bought them all, and he called an hour later and told me they had all sold out. I was like — whoa!"

This was August of '94. Mark used all organic ingredients, including milk, springwater, fresh fruits, nuts, and herbs. The next day the coffee shop guy called for another order. From there Mark expanded to other coffee shops and started using his bike to deliver the donuts. "You see, I had no money," he says. "I couldn't take the subway or a cab, so I put it on the bicycle.

"I had a roommate in my apartment, and after a few weeks of this, the whole apartment had flour and sugar and butter everywhere,"

Mark Isreal celebrates a hometown team's success with the Yankee pin striped doughnut.

he says. "I used my grandfather's recipe, but the idea for the glazes with the fresh fruit and the nuts, that was my contribution. I did raspberry, I mixed in fresh raspberry, and orange with orange zest." He told his roommate that he was going to try Balducci's, "and he laughed at me. 'What are you doing at Balducci's? It's this really big food store!' I walked in there with a box of donuts and I said, 'I make these donuts that I sold to two coffee shops, would you like to try them?' He ate one and he said, 'Wait right here. Can you bring these tomorrow?' and I was like, Okay. Balducci's got to be a big customer."

Next Mark says he thought, "I'm going to really challenge this, I'm going to Dean and DeLuca. And I went to the manager and he bought them on the spot. And he said, 'Can you bring them tomorrow?' Their order was so big that I couldn't do Balducci's and the coffee shop."

The next move was to get out of the apart-

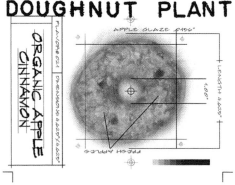

ment, so Isreal told his landlord that he had no money, but, he said, "I need like a storefront or something. I'm going crazy in my apartment, there's donuts everywhere, there's like flour . . . it's crazy. My landlord said, 'I have this boiler room in the basement, it's nothing, I'll give it to you.' So I moved to the basement. It took a month to build it out, with a fryer and fans. My father came to help. . . . It's hard to think about how hard I worked. I was crying all the time."

I ask Mark, "You were one of the first to make donuts that burst out of the traditional, nothing-happening mold?"

"I started in '94, he says, "Krispy Kreme came in '98. And then later people started putting donuts on their menus. But there was nothing going on with donuts then. A few stores said, 'We won't take a donut.' They wouldn't even try them because they had this idea that it was like junk food. And I was like, 'My donuts are different, I use fresh fruit and nuts, it's a whole different vision.' They were like, 'I don't care, we're not gonna have a donut in here, okay?' They thought donuts were trash."

So without any intention of doing so, Mark started the ball rolling for the "new donut," organic and exotic, part of the new food movement, part of the health food movement, part of the gourmet food movement. He turned a fast-food item into a creation with farmers' market ingredients.

"Being alone was good, though," he says. I didn't have my grandfather to teach me, so I learned everything there was about the donut. I was just alone, Me and the Donut!"

Now Mark has a helper: "My name is Haraka. From Trinidad. I'm Indian. I used to do this in Trinidad, I worked in a pastry shop and I used to walk with a basket on the street. That's how I saved enough money to come to America. We made soya pies and jam tarts and coconut tarts. We got donuts there too."

The Doughnut Plant has spiced apple donuts and pumpkin donuts and ginger donuts and poppy seed donuts. Mark: "I like the banana pecan, and the pistachio doughnut, that's probably my most famous. Rose petal is for Mother's Day and Valentine's Day. You know what one of my favorites is? The roasted chestnut. We roast our own chestnuts and scoop them out. It's a lot of work but it's so good. We have a Yankee Doughnut, a World Series donut, with blueberry pinstripes."

Next to the trays of donuts are little signs that are architectural diagrams of the donut, factory blueprints, with dimensions and measuring lines and ingredients. This is an inspired logo, original in its use of another symbolic language, lines and measurements, to apply to this immeasurable American edible. And it ties in with the "plant" motif. Mark says, "It's like a blueprint for the doughnut, you know, the 'doughnut plant' idea."

Mark talks about the satisfactions of his work: "What keeps me going are the customers. They say, 'I woke up this morning just to eat your doughnut.' It is something I never experienced."

He has been in this shop since '99. "I start at midnight, but the guys start the dough at nine at night. We usually sell out. The doughnuts are two dollars. My wholesale business is filled up. Dean and DeLuca, Balducci's, Citarella, Zabar's, coffee shops."

The Doughnut Plant recently opened a store in Japan. Otherwise, there's only one shop, on the Lower East Side of New York. It has been featured in all the media, including a PBS program by Molly O'Neill.

Mark says he thought about doing something in honor of his mother after she died: "I was thinking my mother used to love flowers, so I was like, why not put edible flowers on the doughnuts? I made a glaze of rose petals and rose water, and people like that. In honor of my mother."

DOUGHNUT PLANT CREATIONS
Down-home coconut (above left) and gold-covered luxe (above).

DOUGHNUT PLANT
The Doughnut Plant on NYC's Lower East Side rubs elbows with artists and Hasidim and street people.

The shop's name came from his mother too. "My father used to work in a clothing factory in North Carolina. My mother would say, 'Have a good day at the plant.' So I was like, the Doughnut Plant, the plant, the plant, you know, like factory."

The shop is decorated with a clay relief of donuts made by Mark's father. "My father is a potter, and he had an appreciation for things done by hand. I never liked shortcuts or things done by machine. So when I saw *doughnut* spelled the original way . . . "

These donuts are New York, with their organic ingredients, their funky flavors, their origins in an immigrant Jewish past, their shop location on the Lower East Side, where Jews from Old Europe came to live and where artists live now. Rose petal, chestnut, pistachio — perhaps our ancestors would be turning in their graves, or maybe wishing they had thought of it. Some of Mark's customers are the Goldman Sachs, Smith Barney, and Merrill Lynch offices nearby.

Mark calls his large donuts "New York Big." They are like fluffy pillows you can sink into or, in this case, sink your teeth into. They are a different thing, these donuts of biblical nuts and fruits. Visions of fields and nut trees and fruit-laden orchards drift into my head.

I taste the Mexican churro, and then I float out onto Essex Street, where my ancestors and Mark's too came to tenements and to the old ornate synagogues from the Old World. I float out on a sugar high from the shop of this descendant of a Finnish Jew, a baker in North Carolina, who inspired his grandson to escape from the grid of subjugation by work into the freedom of roaming the streets on his bicycle with boxes of donuts made from Grandpa's recipe, enhanced with farmers' market organic rose petals and raspberries, seeing if people would like them, and they did.

Penn Station, New York. Rain and thunder outside.

The girl from Bangladesh sells donuts at a counter next to pizza. I order a whole wheat donut. She gives me a donut that is yellow inside, with no particular taste. I am thinking, Everything tastes a bit like something else, so you can't blame it for anything. Some donuts are going the way of assimilation, like New York street fairs — they used to be ethnic and now they are "multiethnic," with ubiquitous cheap goods sold by immigrants from everywhere.

I ask her, Is this whole wheat? She says yes. But it's not. Then she gives me another one, tacitly acknowledging the first may not have been what I asked for. This one is brown, very sweet, and not whole wheat-y. On the donuts in the case, the icing is rutted, fissured, "distressed."

GEORGE MAVROTHALASSITIS
The Apotheosis of the Malassada

Hawaii's famous chef Mavro, says, "You know the malassadas are very popular in Hawaii. Local people in the afternoon, they need to relax, they stop by Leonard's, the malassada place, and they buy malassadas in a box and they come back to their offices and they eat malassadas. There are lots of Hawaiians with Portuguese ancestors. The malassada is totally delicious. I've had it since five years ago when I opened the restaurant."

The chef has a deep, hearty voice and a laugh that embodies joie de vivre. He laughs often. Why wouldn't he? Everything he touches turns to . . . stars and diamonds, awards from everywhere, including a 2003 James Beard Award as Best Chef Northwest/Hawaii.

Chef Mavro invented this elegant passion fruit malassada as a variation on Hawaii's donut icon and favorite snack.

Chef Mavro's real name is George Mavrothalassitis. He spent his early life in Marseille. Then he traveled across the ocean to America, where he left a trail of accolades in his wake. Now he has his own elegant restaurant in Hawaii called Chef Mavro, where he creates regional cuisine out of fresh Hawaiian ingredients artfully combined. The favorite dessert on his menu is — a donut! It's a passion fruit–curd-filled beignet, with guava coulis and pineapple-coconut ice cream. He cannot take his distinctive version of the malassada off the menu. It is too popular.

"The malassada started at the Four Seasons Hotel, in '95. I was doing small malassadas filled with lilikoi curd and I was using the fried donut recipe, the real recipe for malassadas. When I opened Mavro, I decided to feature this as a dessert. But of course it was not possible in a restaurant like mine to use a fried donut recipe. So my pastry chef, Jeff Walters, had the idea to use brioche dough. We have people who don't care for gourmet, they come for dessert after the dinner service just to eat malassadas."

He says he does regional cuisine, "with what I find in the market. I use ginger and lemongrass and tamarind and Thai curry."

I ask him if he will stay in Hawaii, considering his previous wanderings.

"I am here to stay for the rest of my life. I love it. I am home."

Lilikoi Malassadas with Guava Coulis

This fancy version of a malassada, created by Pastry Chef Jeff Walters for Chef Mavro restaurant, uses the local flavors of passion fruit (lilikoi) and guava. *Makes 12–15 malassadas*

MALASSADAS

    3 cups bread flour
    ¼ cup sugar, plus more for rolling
    1 tablespoon plus ½ teaspoon dry yeast
    7 eggs
    2 teaspoons salt
    12 ounces butter, softened
       Vegetable oil for frying
       Lilikoi curd
       Guava Coulis
       Vanilla ice cream

1. Mix the flour, sugar, and yeast in an electric mixer with a dough hook. Add about two of the eggs to form a firm paste. Mix on medium speed. Add the remaining eggs one by one, mix the dough for 15 more minutes, and add the salt. Add the softened butter in three parts.

2. Let the dough rise at room temperature, then refrigerate for 2 hours. Form the dough into 12 to 15 balls and let them rise again.

3. Heat the oil to 375°F and fry the malassadas. Drain on paper towels. Roll in sugar.

4. With a pastry bag, fill the malassadas with the Lilikoi Curd.

5. Serve with the Guava Coulis and vanilla ice cream.

LILIKOI CURD

    1 cup sugar
    4 ounces butter
       Juice of ½ lemon
    ¼ cup unsweetened lilikoi concentrate
    6 egg yolks

1. Mix the sugar, butter, lemon, and lilikoi in a saucepan and bring to a boil. In a bowl, whip the yolks with part of the hot liquid, then pour the yolk mixture into the saucepan with the liquid.

2. Return to simmer and keep whipping until the edges start to bubble (do not bring to a full boil). Strain and chill.

GUAVA COULIS

    1 cup simple syrup (half water, half sugar)
    1 cup guava concentrate

Bring the syrup to a boil. Mix together the syrup and guava concentrate.

**EXPRESSIONS FOR
DONUTS AND COFFEE**
Sinkers and Suds
Submarines and a Mug of Murk
. . . No Cow (if coffee is black)
Slugs and Whistle

DREESEN'S FAMOUS DONUTS

It is a perfect, clear, cold November day, a great day for donuts. At Dreesen's in East Hampton, Long Island, the shop that started as a butcher shop and turned into a donut shop too, the "donut robot" is busy making fresh donuts in the window.

Rudy DeSanti, the owner, is a hail-fellow-well-met type. Everybody who comes in the shop kisses him hello and he kisses each of them back. It's a love fest. The donuts are plopping out of the machine, which is small enough to fit in the window, so that everyone who passes can watch them coming. This is an East Hampton institution.

"I wanna start at what I consider the beginning," Rudy says. "In 1948 my father and a partner bought out Dreesen's Excelsior Market Inc. That was a simple, old-fashioned, sawdust-on-the-floor butcher shop with marble counters and beautiful butcher blocks and tin ceilings with porcelain-sculpted walls and round mirrors, absolutely stunning, and a maple wooden–face walk-in refrigerator with the old trapdoor in the top where they used to shove blocks of ice in. That was refrigeration in the old days. They built them with cork and seaweed and tin troughs that would collect the drippings from the ice and run it down on a gravity-fed thing to another trough that dripped into the basement. Isn't that beautiful, the way that is?"

Rudy takes me to see a warren of kitchens and cold storage spaces. In the meat lockers are cuts of meat hanging, beautiful-looking meat. Dreesen's is still the butcher shop it always was but it has also become renowned for Dreesen's Famous Donuts.

Celebrities come into the shop frequently. Rudy says, "Alec Baldwin comes in the store, and one of his lady actress friends on the street waves, and they do a big twirl-around dance step and he kisses her on the lips. My father happened to be there, and he says, 'Sonny, if you need any help, you come to Poppa.'"

There's lots of action in here today, even though East Hampton is a summer place on the ocean, and traffic thins in the fall and winter. But you'd never know that to look at the people discussing turkey orders for Thanksgiving and getting donuts hot from the fryer. The place is not fancy; it's very basic, old-fashioned, with a homey feeling about it. Rudy's son Rudy, a Culinary Institute chef, is there too. It's clear that people love the atmosphere, they love the meat and the donuts, and they love the Rudys.

The family came to Sag Harbor from the village of Ginestra Sabina in the mountains near Rome in the early 1900s. "My grandfather came over alone and worked in a brickyard in Sag Harbor on Brick Kiln Road. He became a foreman. They had a little one-room

The Rudys at Dreesen's in Sag Harbor, N.Y., where their donuts delight celebrities and townspeople.

shack that the foreman had and a horse and wagon. They would make bricks all day and deliver them all night. We have four generations of Rudys.

"My grandfather had a main job on Shelter Island. Every day he would take his horse or cart, and he would go down to the channel to get to Shelter Island. And listen to this — my grandfather would light a lantern and hoist it up a twelve-foot pole. Old Mr. Clark would wave a lantern, get in his rowboat, row across the channel, put my grandfather and the bicycle in the boat, lower the lantern, blow it out, and row him across, and he, my grandfather, would get on his bike and go to work. He was the caretaker in Shelter Island. That's how they started the ferryboats in Sag Harbor. His name was — are you ready for this? — Sabatino DeSanti. My son is a chef,

and one day he's going to open a restaurant, and it will be Sabatino's."

Rudy is a great raconteur. He tells the story of how the butcher shop began to sell donuts: "In the forties and fifties, there was a five-and-dime in East Hampton, and they had a machine there that was like a big square drum, and they would plunk this donut batter into it and turn it over with drumsticks. I still have that machine on a shelf in the back room. It's just a dear thing to have. The donuts at the five-and-dime were absolutely very nice. He did it to get people to come in the door. His name was Mr. Frank Brill, a lovely man, he looked like Santa Claus. It's the only way to describe Mr. Brill, the beard, the chubbiness. The five-and-dime is a ladies' underwear store now, whaddya gonna do? C'est la vie, as the French say."

He says that Mr. Brill decided to get rid of the donut machine, which was the kind that just "cut and plopped." At the same time, someone offered Rudy's father an automatic machine, a Donut Robot, made by the Belshaw Company: "It turned it, it drained it, it plopped it, it did the whole works. Eight hundred fifty-five dollars. He stood there and made them all day to teach you. For that kind of money in those days that was a big thing. Okay? So now we have a donut machine, and the store has not changed resemblance to what it had been for years much to this point. These are fir, oiled floors topped with pine sawdust. The donut machine was to bring people into the store, and it was doing its job wonderfully."

Then in the '60s, Rudy got out of the service and went into building houses. In 1970 his father's partner died. "My father said the store is closed for good, I can't go there anymore, I have too many memories." So Rudy offered to run the store while his parents went to Florida to decide what to do. "My father came back and he said, 'I don't want to run the store, what do you think about it?' And I said, 'I like it.' I really always did like it. I've done that since 1970. It was a meat shop with donuts, that's all it was."

Over time it became a full deli, and the donut business also mushroomed. "The donuts developed and developed," Rudy says. "We do about 24,000 dozen a year, just in my store. We have twenty-five stores. They buy equipment from me and put it in their window, and they sell my product made to my specifications, and they keep the profit. There's the Bagel Buoy in Sag Harbor, Cassel's Farm Stand in Watermill, Westhampton Beach Country Club, and in New York, Tavern on the Green at brunch, Balthazar's, Schiller's . . ."

Rudy makes ice cream with donut chunks in it and donut pudding with leftover crumbled donuts. He has developed kits for home donut making, and even a cart with a donut machine on it that made donuts for 500 for a Bat Mitzvah. And, he says, "I had this guy

A VARIATION ON THE OPTIMIST'S CREED
An American writer, McLandburgh Wilson, wrote in 1915:
"Twixt optimist and pessimist
The difference is droll:
The optimist sees the doughnut,
The pessimist, the hole."

make a big donut head, it's a face and you can put it on your head. I have some kids working for me, and I have them wear it around the street giving out donuts."

When Rudy talks, you hear that he has taken himself by surprise, creating this original venture that has caught fire. "I decided maybe there was something about the donuts," he says. "We make my own recipe, blended in a mill. On 9/12 after 9/11, we got some white coconut and blue dye and red dye. We dip it in white and red and blue, and we sprinkle the center with white so we make red, white, and blue donuts, and we still do that."

In the back are piles of large sacks of Dreesen's Famous Donut Mix, which Rudy concocted himself. "The trick was just the right amount of nutmeg," he says. "We locked the recipe in the safe, and that's the recipe we work with today. We got lucky, we were a couple of dummies. I'm a butcher."

Krispy Kreme has created the last word in wedding cakes, and they have become trendy. They almost led to a riot at one wedding.

MARCUS SAMUELSSON

Creator of the Green Tea Donut

Marcus Samuelsson, the famous Ethiopian chef who was raised in Sweden and is now considered one of New York's best chefs, has just come up with a brainstorm creation, a green tea donut for his new restaurant, Riingo, which combines Japanese and American influences.

Samuelsson says, "It was a creation I came up with when I was thinking about what is one of the most American desserts/breads — donuts! And, then, what is the most interesting Japanese ingredient? Green tea! I wanted to come up with a creative way to mesh the two cultures together in a fun dish."

Marcus Samuelsson is the chef of Aquavit, a very successful Scandinavian restaurant in Manhattan. He was born in Ethiopia, orphaned, adopted by a Swedish couple, and grew up in Sweden with his Swedish grandmother, the cook for a rich family, as his model in the kitchen. Aquavit fuses Scandinavian cuisine with elements like the exotic spices of Asia and Africa that inform the smoked salmon. Amazing, even slightly shocking, combinations show up — vegetable purées perfumed with mustard, for example.

The new restaurant is named Riingo, the word for apple in Japanese. It features Samuelsson's original take on both Japanese and American cuisine, just as his clothes are his original take on apparel. As a belt he wears a seat belt from American Airlines. The green tea donut is an unprecedented mix of cultures and flavors and influences. It is made with potatoes and injected with "green tea jam" — in which there is no green tea but rather edamame (green soy beans) and yuzu (a Japanese citrus fruit) juice. It is accompanied by a cinnamon sabayon, green tea kulfi (a milky sauce made with green tea powder), and a chutney of exotic fresh and dried fruits and spices. Preserved lemon, dried cranberries, fresh quince, and green and black cardamom pods and fenugreek seeds are some of the elements. Strange bedfellows, but Samuelsson has a knack for making seemingly outlandish combinations that work.

"I wanted America to meet Japan," he says. "It's all about shapes, lines. The focal point is the green tea donut. Boom! That's the star of it all." And a word of approval for his creation, "This is killer."

Green Tea Donuts

The green tea donut was created by Marcus Samuelsson for his new restaurant, Riingo, where Japan meets America. Samuelsson's specialty is combining culinary traditions to produce unexpected creations, like this donut that nobody else could have invented. *Makes about 1 dozen donuts*

DONUT

- 3½ cups milk
- 1 cup sugar
- 8 ounces butter (2 sticks)
- 1 ounce fresh yeast
- ½ cup warm water
- 1 cup white rum
- 4 eggs
- 4 pounds, 2 ounces flour (about 15 cups)
- 1½ tablespoons salt
- 2 teaspoons baking powder
- 1 cup potatoes (boiled, rinsed, and mashed)
- Vegetable oil for frying

1. In a saucepan, bring the milk, sugar, and butter to a boil. Set aside.

2. Dissolve the yeast in water. When the milk mixture is room temperature, add the dissolved yeast, rum, and eggs to it. Mix well in an electric mixer. Add the flour, salt, baking powder, and potatoes. Knead to a soft dough with a dough hook. Remove the dough. Place in an oiled container and let it rest for 4 hours covered.

3. Roll the dough on a floured surface and cut into desired shapes. Place them on greased parchment paper. Let them rest for 1 hour.

4. Heat the oil to 350°F and fry the donuts until a golden color. Drain them on paper towels, then toss in flavored sugar.

GREEN TEA JAM

- 3 pounds edamame
- 1 cup sugar
- 6 tablespoons yuzu juice
- 1 cup apricot jam

1. Boil the edamame until they are soft. Peel.

2. Purée peeled edamame in a blender with the sugar and yuzu juice. Add the rest of the ingredients and pass the mixture through a ricer. Refrigerate.

CINNAMON SABAYON

12 egg yolks

⅔ cup milk

¾ cup sugar

1½ teaspoons ground cinnamon

½ teaspoon rum

1. In a bowl, combine all ingredients. Whisk until thick and creamy over a double boiler.

2. Remove from heat and cool to room temperature by whisking the sabayon in an electric mixer.

GREEN TEA KULFI

1 can (14 ounces) condensed milk

4 cups heavy cream

2 cups evaporated milk

¼ cup green tea powder

1. In a saucepan, bring the first three ingredients to a boil. Simmer for 8 minutes, then add the green tea powder.

2. Strain, pour in a mold, and freeze.

SWEET FRUIT CHUTNEY

2 tablespoons oil

1 teaspoon fenugreek seeds

4 green cardamom pods

2 black cardamom pods

2 bay leaves

2 cinnamon sticks

3½ cups diced fresh fruit (apples, figs, plums, pears, semiripe mango, quince)

½ cup dark brown sugar

½ cup light brown sugar

½ cup sugar

1 tablespoon diced lemon confit

½ cup dry fruit (tart cherries, golden raisins, cranberries)

1 tablespoon yuzu juice

¼ cup toasted almond slivers

1. Heat the oil and add all the spices.

2. Add the fresh fruit and cook for 5 minutes. Add all the sugars. Cook until the fruit is tender.

3. Add the lemon confit and dried fruits. Cook for 2 minutes, then add the yuzu juice.

4. Remove the mixture from the heat and fold in the toasted almonds.

ASSEMBLY

1. With a pastry bag and plain tip, insert the Green Tea Jam into a donut.

2. Put the donut in the middle of a plate and arrange the Cinnamon Sabayon, Sweet Fruit Chutney, and Green Tea Kulfi around it.

GLIMPSES OF KRISPY KREME: SUGAR IN MY BLOOD!

I head toward the Krispy Kreme Penn Station shop. There's a long line. Everyone is in full tilt about his or her favorite donut. With its Christmas colors, the shop is spotless, open to the world, at least to those riding the rails. There is a Latin American family with lots of kids. They all want glazed. The donuts are puffed, shining, splendid. Each one is perfect, not collapsed or messy. The donuts look as new as newborn babies in a nursery. The chocolate is glistening, with a sheen like newly frosted hair. The donuts are alluring rings with shining colored crowns of icing, sheer white of gauzy silk, baby blanket pink.

The people are not just waiting for the donuts; they are talking about the donuts.

"You want your Boston Crème, Mommy?"

"Yeah," she says and turns to me. "I don't eat them much, but when I have one, that's the one I like."

The kids can't wait for theirs, all glazed.

"Hey, what kind you want?"

Glazed, glazed, glazed.

I ask for the plainest variety. It's a ring with a dusting of sugar. For a chain shop

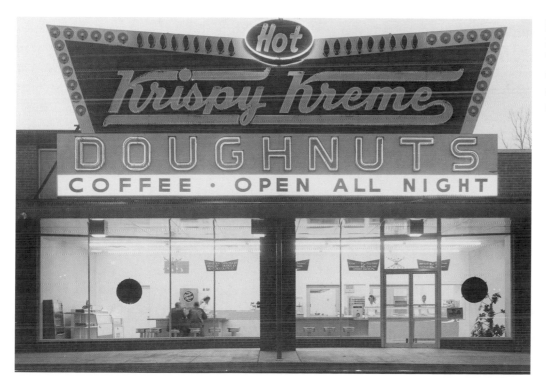

NIGHT LIGHT
Krispy Kreme's "hot light" has crowds lining up all night before a shop opens.

donut, it's everything a donut should be. Eighty-four cents.

It's still raining, the trains are running, people are eating, especially donuts. Especially Krispy Kreme, the flavor of now.

Krispy Kreme is on the march. It has made it to Australia. And to the stratosphere of donut consciousness. Jack McAleer, Krispy Kreme executive, tells his version of the Krispy Kreme story:

The story is at the store. Especially when they first experience a hot one — oh my goodness! I have to tell you that when we get to a market we haven't been in before, because of all the hoopla among our passionate fans, people go nuts. The night before opening there's always a line that forms and they share stories. The next morning, when the hot light trips on and everybody gets their first hot donut on the house, the line can be as long as an hour, two hours long. When I ask if they have had a hot Krispy Kreme before, and if they haven't I say, you are standing in this line and you don't even know why you are standing in the line! They bite in and the knees buckle and the mmmmm, and so then . . . wow! And then we talk to them about our neon sign, the red glow, hot now. It gets people talking. Then I'll have a customer tell the next customer about it, and it's just fun.

In an article called "The Hole Story," in *Fortune* magazine, Andy Serwer writes, "With so many companies today desperate for customers, here is a business — remember, we're talking donuts — that has shrieking fanatics lining up around the block in the middle of the night to buy its product."

What is it that makes Krispy Kreme different? McAleer says, "At the core is that it transcends the donut. It's the experience surrounding the donut. So many great stories that we hear every day of how people came together around donuts." From Stan, the donut pitchman, to Krispy Kreme, people will always gather around donuts.

Krispy Kreme has started a foundation project based on storytelling and its value in learning. It takes its cue from the fact that at every store opening people tell their donut stories. The company happened on a storytelling festival in Tennessee, at the International Storytelling Center in Jonesboro, which is linked to Harvard and the Smithsonian. They started working with senior high school students, based on the conviction that the best way to communicate is through stories. "When you tell it in a story format, people learn and are engaged. We see it as applying to business and education and family structure or church," says McAleer.

McAleer tells his own story of memories of his father's Krispy Kreme shop. "I was mesmerized by the donut equipment. At the time they were using a donut table with a rolling pin that stamped out the donuts and I remember they would pick out those holes and anything I could do to get over and pick out those holes, just to get your hands in that dusting flour and the dough. I was five or six. So . . . I grew up in it, Sugar in My Blood!"

McAleer's father had been in the business from the ground up, starting in Mobile, Alabama, as an early franchisee, after working in a billiard hall for his father, and then in a shipyard: "He saw an ad in the want ads to open a donut shop, and they had just opened a store in Pensacola. The owner [of Krispy Kreme], Vernon Rudolph, said, 'You can have the franchise in Mobile but you have to come and work in Pensacola for six months,' which he did. That started him in the Krispy Kreme business, so he opened in Mobile."

Jack McAleer was the sixth of seven kids. By the time he was out of college, Krispy Kreme had been sold to Beatrice Foods, in 1976, after the founder died in 1973. In 1982, Jack McAleer's father put together a group of franchisees to buy back the business from Beatrice, which had not been a good match. "It went back into the hands of the people that knew the heart and soul of the business. They understood the product and the brand," says McAleer.

What is a Krispy Kreme donut? Here's how Jack McAleer tells it:

"The name Krispy Kreme had everything

to do with the way the product was made originally. The original formula was all raw ingredients and they made a cream base of potatoes and sugar and milk. The cream base is where the 'Kreme' part comes from. And as it was fried lightly, it left a crispy crunch on the skin of the donut. It came from a French recipe. Vernon Rudolph's uncle Ishmael Armstrong met a man in Paducah, Kentucky,

SERVICE WITH A SMILE
Krispy Kreme, which started as a small donut shop, now has outposts across America and throughout the world.

in 1933, who had this recipe and the name. Ishmael Armstrong bought the recipe and name from Joe Le Beau."

Ishmael Armstrong was a farmer. The first recipe was handwritten on a paper napkin. In 1937, Vernon Rudolph went to Winston-Salem, North Carolina, with a friend, $25, and an old Pontiac, which they used as a delivery van. They rented the front of a store and the owner lent them donut ingredients. The smell attracted customers, so Rudolph punched out a hole in the shop, and this turned into the idea of watching the donuts being made while breathing in the aroma. Today Krispy Kreme calls this "Doughnut Theater."

Jack McAleer worked with his father and in corporate headquarters, and then managed the Winston-Salem store. "My favorite place to be was out on the front line talking to customers about the hot light and putting a selection of donuts together, so they would have a great experience."

He says, "My brother came up with the idea of turning the equipment perpendicular with the street so we could bring a curve of donuts out into the front of the store. This was a real turning point. We had always had a plate-glass window showing off the production, even from Vernon's first store in Old Salem. Then it was just the pot and the wooden stick, so we enhanced that to create Doughnut Theater. Donuts are the focal point and we are the supporting cast."

Then McAleer started to think about franchising, and he picked Indianapolis, where there was only 2 percent awareness of Krispy Kreme, compared to 99 percent in North Carolina. "The most important thing we did was bring donuts to the media," he says. "We told them there were hot donuts now. We got a call from a local celebrity, a TV personality, his dog's name was Barney. He asked if he could say that if they came by the shop, they would get a free dozen glazed if they mentioned his dog's name. We said okay.

"Lo and behold, the nine percent became bigger and there were fans that couldn't wait to tell us a story. I took ten dozen to the studio and it was five in the morning and the guard wouldn't let me in. I said, Have you ever had Krispy Kreme and he said no. We got our fans to be our ambassadors. Not a better way to sell than to have someone passionate about it do it for you." Krispy Kreme has found that giving away free donuts works better than advertising.

Then Krispy Kreme exploded, moving into New York and all over the country and into the rest of the world. McAleer says, "We treated New York like any other market, and what happened was the local media were the national media. Instead of this man with his dog Barney, it was Katie Couric. We were getting offers to be in movies and TV. We were just this little donut shop, really."

Krispy Kreme Shop, West 72nd Street, New York City, July 4 weekend, 2003. Late afternoon, hot and sunny.

I had just come from Le Pain Quotidien, a small French pastry shop with a fresh cream donut, to Krispy Kreme, a different world. Krispy Kreme is America, an everybody place.

On the door is a poster showing the special donut of the day, the Key Lime Pie donut, with crumb top and white icing.

Inside are donuts with colored sprinkles, and there's Darry, the counter guy, ready for his photo op. Two hefty women inside the glass-enclosed baking area load donut cooling trays with donuts hot off the fryer. Round puffed-up donuts nicely browned on top have just the right air-blown look to them. They are raw material, just fried, not filled yet. There's a "community bulletin board" with a photo of kids in a class.

Darry smiles next to the tray of hot donuts and says, "Will I be in the book?"

The shop has as wallpaper enlarged photos of old wooden Krispy Kreme shops back in history.

Historically, donuts have a mission, mending fences, uniting. E pluribus unum, it's Independence Day, justice — and donuts — for all.

Krispy Kreme has become the brand that represents the original icon, the donut. The phrase "Krispy Kreme" even replaces *donut* in terminology used in George Johnson's *New York Times* article describing the shape of the universe. It speaks of the "Krispy Kreme universe in all its glory," its shape "a kind of hyper-doughnut."

North American Shops

ALL STAR DONUTS
2095 Chestnut Street
San Francisco, California
415-441-9270

ALLIE'S DONUT SHOP
3661 Quaker Lane
North Kingstown, Rhode Island
401-295-8036

ANNA'S HAND CUT DONUTS
2056 Centre Street
West Roxbury, Massachusetts
617-323-2680

BEACH DONUT SHOP
(formerly of Old Lyme, Connecticut)

BOB'S DONUTS
1621 Polk Street
San Francisco, California
415-776-3141

CAFÉ DU MONDE
New Orleans, Louisiana
800-772-2927
www.cafedumonde.com
Several metro locations

CARL'S DONUTS
6350 Sunset Corporate Drive
Las Vegas, Nevada
702-382-6138
http://carlsdonuts.com

CHUCK'S DO-NUT SHOP
(formerly of Denver, Colorado)

COFFEE AN' DONUT SHOP
343 Main Street
Westport, Connecticut
203-227-3808

CONGDON'S DONUTS
1090 Post Road
Wells, Maine
207-646-4219
http://congdons.com

CUPCAKE CAFÉ
545 9th Avenue
New York, New York
212-268-9975
www.cupcakecafe-nyc.com

DAYLIGHT DONUTS
800-331-2245
www.daylightdonuts.com
All over

DOUGHNUT PLANT
379 Grand Street
New York, New York
212-505-3700
www.doughnutplant.com

THE DONUT HOLE
15300 Amar Road
La Puente, California
626-968-2912

DREESEN'S FAMOUS DONUTS
www.dreesens.com
Many locations in New York City, plus a
few others elsewhere

DUNKIN' DONUTS
www.dunkindonuts.com
All over

FERRELL'S DONUT SHOP
(formerly of Santa Cruz, California)

**FLAKY CREAM DO-NUTS &
COFFEE SHOP**
441 Center Street
Healdsburg, California
707-433-3895

FRACTURED PRUNE
www.fracturedprune.com
All over the U.S. East Coast

**IGGY'S DOUGHBOYS &
CHOWDER HOUSE**
889 Oakland Beach Avenue
Warwick, Rhode Island
401-737-9459
www.iggysdoughboys.com
One of two locations

KING PIN DONUTS
2521 Durant Avenue
Berkeley, California
510-843-6688

KRISPY KREME DOUGHNUTS
www.krispykreme.com
All over

LAMAR'S DONUTS
www.lamars.com
All over the mid–United States

LEONARD'S BAKERY
933 Kapahulu Avenue
Honolulu, Hawaii
808-737-5591
www.leonardshawaii.com
One of two metro locations

LONE STAR BAKERY
(see Round Rock Donuts, Ltd)

MCDONALD'S
18 E. 42nd Street
New York, New York
www.mcnewyork.com/25696
(and formerly of 151 W. 34th Street
New York, New York)

MECHE'S DONUT KING
7259 Highway 182 E.
Morgan City, Louisiana
985-384-0358

MRS. MURPHY'S DONUTS
374 Depot Street
Manchester Center, Vermont
802-362-1874

MUSTANG DONUTS
6601 Hillcrest Avenue
Dallas, Texas
214-363-4878

NEVILLE'S DO-NUT SHOP
(formerly of North Adams,
Massachusetts)

NOTHING BUT DONUTS
50 Massachusetts Avenue NE
Union Station
Washington, D.C.
202-408-9464

ON THE AVENUE DONUTS
(formerly of Gaithersburg,
Maryland)

THE ORCHARDS OF CONCKLIN
2 South Mountain Road
Pomona, New York
845-354-0369
www.orchardsofconcklin.com

PRESTI'S
(formerly of Cleveland, Ohio)

RANDY'S DONUTS
805 West Manchester Avenue
Inglewood, California
310-645-4707
http://randys-donuts.com

RAYMOND'S DONUT SHOP
(formerly of Tulsa, Oklahoma)

ROUND ROCK DONUTS, LTD.
106 West Liberty Street
Round Rock, Texas
512-255-3629
www.roundrockdonuts.com

SNOWFLAKE DONUT SHOP
(formerly of Incline Village, Nevada)

SNOWFLAKE DONUTS
(formerly Southern Maid Donuts of
Houston, Texas)

STAN'S CORNER DOUGHNUT SHOP
10948 Weyburn Avenue
Westwood Village, California
310-208-8660
www.stansdoughnuts.com

TIM HORTONS
www.timhortons.com
All over Canada and along the U.S.
East Coast

VERNA'S COFFEE & DONUT SHOP
2344 Massachusetts Avenue
Cambridge, Massachusetts
617-354-4110
www.vernaspastry.com

WORLD'S BEST DONUTS
10 E. Wisconsin Street
Grand Marais, Minnesota
218-387-1345
http://worldsbestdonutsmn.com

ZIGGY'S DONUTS
2 Essex Street
Salem, Massachusetts
978-744-9605

Abroad

BEACHES
St.-Tropez, France

BE-BOULANGEPICIER
Paris, France
www.boulangepicier.com

DUNKIN' DONUTS
www.dunkindonuts.com
Worldwide

KRISPY KREME
www.krispykreme.com
Worldwide

NANNINI
Siena, Italy
www.grupponannini.it

INTERIOR CREDITS

PHOTOGRAPHY CREDITS

Index

Page numbers in italic refer to illustrations.